PUBLIC INTEREST LOBBIES

D1253225

PUBLIC INTEREST LOBBIES

Decision making on energy

Andrew S. McFarland

WITHDRAWN

LIBRARY
OF
MOUNT ST. MARY'S
COLLEGE
EMMITSBURG, MARYLAND

Andrew S. McFarland holds a grant from the Ford Foundation to write a book about Common Cause.

Library of Congress Cataloging in Publication Data

McFarland, Andrew S   1940–
    Public interest lobbies.

    (National energy study; 14)   (AEI studies; 136)
    1. Energy Policy—United States.   2. Pressure
groups—United States.   I. Title.   II. Series.
III. Series: American Enterprise Institute for
Public Policy Research. AEI studies; 136.
HD9502.U52M32   333.7   76-51340
ISBN 0-8447-3229-X

© 1976 by American Enterprise Institute for Public Policy Research, Washington, D.C. Permission to quote from or to reproduce materials in this publication is granted when due acknowledgment is made.

Printed in the United States of America

CONTENTS

ACKNOWLEDGMENTS

I wish to thank Gilbert Steiner and the friendly personnel of the Governmental Studies Program at the Brookings Institution for their kind hospitality while I wrote this volume as part of a more extensive project. In addition I wish to thank Ralph Magnus, Marilyn McMorran, Daniel Metlay, Edward Mitchell, and Aaron Wildavsky for assistance in setting up and in implementing this project. This volume is dedicated to my two favorite Southern California commuters—Elizabeth Campbell and Jean Ellen Stearns.

1
THE RISE OF
PUBLIC INTEREST GROUPS:
1965–75

This monograph is concerned with two new elements of the American political scene—public interest groups and the energy crisis. Certainly the concept "public interest" is an ambiguous one. And surely the system of linked, critical policy choices referred to as the energy crisis is complex and multifaceted. It is not immediately clear what public interests might be with respect to energy matters. How, then, do public interest groups decide what goals to pursue in their lobbying and public relations efforts?

I engage this question in the following way. After this introductory discussion of public interest groups, I offer a rationale for their existence within a pluralist democracy according to a theory of interest group formation. I argue that there is indeed a need to represent within the political process interests that are widespread but difficult to organize. (This does not necessarily imply, however, that any particular group or type of group is indeed representing such significant but diffuse interests.) I then examine the stands of six public interest groups—Common Cause, Ralph Nader's Critical Mass, the League of Women Voters, the Sierra Club, the Consumer Federation of America's Energy Policy Task Force, Consumers Union, and a borderline group, Americans for Energy Independence. (Consumers Union and Americans for Energy Independence do not try to influence congressional voting on pending legislation, and thus are not "lobbies" in the legal sense. The other five groups are, legally speaking, lobbies, because they seek to exercise such influence.) I look at their stands in relation to the rationale for the existence of public interest groups and to their organizational structure and the composition of their membership. I note that these groups share a system of beliefs which I call the theory of civic balance—the interests of a few tend to predominate at the expense of the welfare of the many in numerous areas of public policy.

I show that this system of beliefs, in combination with membership composition and organizational structure, tends to determine stands on energy questions. I conclude with observations about the role of public interest groups in current American politics.

Readers who are much more interested in energy questions than in theoretical understanding of political processes will prefer to concentrate their attention on Chapters 3 to 6, which deal with the stands on energy of the groups being considered.

Public Interest Groups: Old or New?

It is easy to waste time arguing whether the present generation of public interest groups is a new phenomenon or merely the latest manifestation of an old phenomenon. Enthusiastic proponents of public interest groups sometimes state or imply that these groups represent an entirely new political force on the American scene—thereby dramatizing the accomplishments of these groups. Critics of public interest groups ordinarily point to the tradition of public interest reform in American politics—the Progressives, generations of proponents of good government, and so forth—and view Common Cause, Nader, and the others as the latest manifestation of this tradition. These critics, whose observations are commonly infused with antagonism, argue that since such reform groups have failed to achieve their goals in the past, the current set of such groups is also bound to fail and therefore need not have much attention paid to them.

The recent upsurge of power on the part of public interest groups is in fact the present manifestation of a tendency in American politics that surely dates back at least to the 1890s. The aims of the public interest movement today are not new: Municipal reformers of the 1890s advocated reforms similar to some of those advocated by Common Cause (ceilings on expenditures in political campaigns, for example), and the Muckrakers of the era 1905–15 exposed corporate infringements of the general public welfare in a way that foreshadowed Nader's dramatic investigatory journalism and public interest research. What is new is the amount of influence that public interest groups have acquired in a relatively short time. Ten years ago environmentalists were still conservationists, Common Cause did not exist, and Ralph Nader was a newcomer on the national political scene.

As evidence of the influence of public interest groups, consider these events of the last decade: A coalition of environmentalist groups delayed the construction of the Alaskan oil pipeline for four years, even though the project was supported by the oil industry and the incumbent administration of the federal government.[1] A group of political unknowns in California succeeded in gaining a majority of 70 percent in support of a referendum which changed the rules for elections and lobbying, despite the opposition of business *and* labor *and* political party leaders.[2] In 1965, the American automobile industry was generally independent of federal regulation. During the last decade that industry has become subject to a great many regulations—with respect to safety equipment, gas mileage, and, increasingly, emissions—and this regulation was precipitated by Nader's exposures of safety defects, exposures which undercut the industry's public prestige.[3] Incessant lobbying efforts by Common Cause, in combination with activity by congressional reformers, have led to restrictions on the financing of political campaigns that could not have been predicted in 1970 or even in 1972 (though perhaps Richard Nixon and Watergate are partly responsible for these reforms).[4] Things have changed since the early 1960s, when cars came without seat belts, no one was concerned about the safety hazards created by nuclear power plants or the land laid waste by strip mining, the Kennedy administration tried to kill legislation introduced by Estes Kefauver to ensure that new drugs were adequately tested before they were prescribed to the public,[5] and neither political scientists nor members of Congress could remember the details of legislation regarding campaign finances, since such laws as were on the books were never enforced.

In the last few years, public interest groups, and the type of public opinion that they express, have been more influential in American politics than at any time since the entry of the United States into the First World War ended the so-called Progressive Era. Like the Progressives, the supporters of the recent public interest movement, whom we shall henceforth call the new civic reformers, come from the white middle classes. According to an internal survey, the average family income in 1974 of the Massachusetts members of Common Cause, a broad-based and generally centrist public interest group, was $20,000. The typical member of Common Cause had been educated beyond the

---

[1] See Mary Clay Berry, *The Alaska Pipeline* (Bloomington: Indiana University Press, 1975); Richard Corrigan, *The Trans-Alaska Pipeline: A Case Study in Energy Politics* (Washington, D.C.: American Enterprise Institute, forthcoming).

[2] See a forthcoming Ph.D. dissertation on Proposition 9 by Ken Smith, Department of Public Administration, University of Southern California. Mr. Smith was one of the principal leaders of the Proposition 9 campaign.

[3] See Paul J. Halpern, "Consumer Politics and Corporate Behavior: The Case of Automobile Safety" (Ph.D. diss., Harvard University, 1972).

[4] See *Congressional Quarterly Almanac*, vol. 30 (1974), pp. 611–33.

[5] J.B. Gorman, *Kefauver: A Political Biography* (New York: Oxford University Press, 1971).

B.A. level. It is my impression that members of other public interest groups would be found to have similar characteristics. (At present it cannot be shown that the new civic reformers are disproportionately Anglo-Saxon Protestant, as were the Progressives.)

How can we understand this tradition of middle-class civic reform in America? What motivated the Progressives? What motivates the civic reformers of today? This has been a puzzle to many observers. Interpretations of politics in terms of economic interests or ethnic, religious, racial, or regional conflict do not usually provide satisfactory explanations of the political behavior of middle-class reformers.

In some cases the motivations of persons who join public interest groups are widely understood. Anyone with an upper middle-class income will surely save many times the $11 price of membership in Consumers Union if he pays attention to the product information reported in that group's journal. The outdoorsman and conservationist can easily recover his $15 Sierra Club dues through reduced-fare travel, hikes, and social get-togethers organized by the club, to say nothing of the fact that the dues include a subscription to the monthly magazine.

But why do 275,000 persons send $15 to $20 a year to Common Cause, when they receive nothing in return but thank-you letters and an eight-page monthly newsletter? The 100,000 persons who send an average of $11 a year to Nader's Public Citizen, Inc., get a five-page progress report and a pamphlet, but no thank-you letter (to save money). At the time of writing, I do not believe that either of the so-called major political parties could persuade 275,000 citizens to contribute $15 to $20. Only a handful of presidential contenders could hope to match the results of Common Cause's solicitation of funds. Common Cause and Public Citizen are evidently attracting their strong support for reasons that are not primarily economic.

Causes of the New Civic Reform Movement

Let us consider seven factors which may help in understanding the increase in the influence of public interest groups in recent years. These are: (1) the increase in middle-class participation in American politics in the 1960s and 1970s; (2) the corresponding increase in the politics of issues and systems of beliefs as opposed to the politics of party identification, personality, or patronage; (3) the growth of "civic skepticism"—the disbelief in the utility of existing politics and public administrative practices in solving important social problems; (4) skillful leadership of public interest groups; (5) technical advances in communications; (6) economic prosperity; and (7) initial success bringing more success.

The Increase of Middle-Class Participation. We might also call this factor the increase of college education in America. Political scientists have demonstrated that the level of a person's education is directly correlated with the extent of his participation in American politics. For example, Sidney Verba and Norman H. Nie found in their nation-wide survey that those with "some college or more" were found twice as often in the group of "complete activists" as would be expected from their proportion in the total sample. Conversely, those with "grade school or less" were found in the activist sample only half as often as would be expected from their proportion of the population.[6] The term *complete activists* designated those who were active in all four types of participation: voting only, political campaigning, activity in community-oriented groups, and making contact with government officials.

Available evidence indicates that supporters of public interest groups generally fall into the 11 percent of the public designated as "complete activists." In a careful survey done for the management of Common Cause, a majority of the supporters of Common Cause in Massachusetts were found to be active in partisan politics. Contribution to one or more public interest groups—multiple contributions are a frequent phenomenon—indicate a particularly high psychological involvement in politics, unless the contribution is to one of those groups who repay their members with financial savings, such as Consumers Union. It seems safe to say that the majority of contributors to Common Cause, Nader, and the environmentalist movement also vote, occasionally try to persuade a friend to vote for a favorite candidate, and communicate with a government official about some matter.

Table 1 indicates the increasing percentage of the total population having some college education. Education increases one's faculty for understanding political communications; the educated person reads more and understands more of what he reads. Education also increases one's faculty for linking distant political events to things one cares about; the educated person sees that abstract controversies about the safety of nuclear power plants may affect his own personal safety and financial resources, that disputes over the disposition of the Panama Canal Zone affect U.S. relations with Latin America and could therefore affect the price of coffee, and so forth.

[6] Sidney Verba and Norman H. Nie, *Participation in America* (New York: Harper & Row, 1972), p. 100.

Table 1

ADULTS AGED 25 AND OVER HAVING SOME
COLLEGE EDUCATION

Year	Percentage
1950	13.4
1960	16.5
1970	21.2
1974	25.2

Source: U.S. Bureau of the Census.

Thus, college education affects the extent of middle-class participation in politics through intervening factors. It increases the psychological involvement of the citizen; he pays more attention to politics and is more interested in what is happening. He gains more information about politics. College education is associated with high income and high social prestige. This is likely to affect a person's sense of political efficacy; he is more confident that political action is an effective way to attain his goals.[7]

Thus, increases in education result in increases in political participation, thereby increasing the numbers of citizens who might donate $15 to a public interest lobby. Since environmentalist, consumer, and good-government groups with large memberships appear to rely primarily on the college educated for support, increases in the numbers of those with higher education are a predisposing factor to the appearance and maintenance of such groups.

The Politics of Issues and Systems of Beliefs. Political scientists conventionally categorize motivations for voting and other political acts according to party identification, attraction to a personality, patronage incentives, and issue orientation.[8] For instance, one who voted for Eisenhower in 1952 might have done so chiefly because the voter was a loyal Republican, or because he was attracted to Eisenhower as a person even though he normally voted Democratic, or because he preferred the Republican candidate's stand on some issue—such as the possibility of ending the Korean War. Patronage has been found to be a factor in local elections; the citizen votes for a politician because of some favor the politician has done for the voter.

Survey research has found that only a small percentage of the

---

[7] Ibid., pp. 125–37.

[8] Angus Campbell, Philip E. Converse, Warren E. Miller, Donald E. Stokes, *The American Voter* (New York: John Wiley & Sons, 1960).

American voting public has been motivated by the issues—about 10 percent in the 1950s.[9] From 1964, however, the frequency of motivation by the issues increased to the point that in 1972 researchers found that issues were more important than party loyalty and almost as important as reactions to the candidates' personalities in the Nixon-McGovern election.[10] The greater frequency of issue voting is probably the result of the fact that there is a greater atmosphere of criticism and debate than there was during the 1950s. But the increasing number of college-educated, middle-class citizens is likely to be another factor producing an increase in the proportion of issue-motivated political actions. The college educated are much more likely to be concerned about issues than those with less education.[11] Until contradictory evidence is found, we can presume that the great majority of contributors to public interest groups (whom we know to be college-educated) have an issue orientation to politics. This is particularly the case if we use *issue orientation* in a broad sense, so that the term includes motivations that are primarily emotional (for example, a feeling of guilt about one's personal treatment of the natural environment that provides the motivation for a contribution to the Environmental Defense Fund).

The world of politics is difficult to understand. Political and social reality is complex: causation is always multiple; it seems as if everything is always related to everything else. If we establish a public policy in response to one situation, it seems that either nothing happens or everything happens, and a hundred other social situations are unpredictably affected. To deal with such social complexity, people resort to systems of beliefs—sets of related ideas which provide a theory of the way in which society works and which may imply a course of action to deal with some problem.[12] Systems of beliefs simplify social reality sufficiently that the individual can deal with it. Systems of beliefs indicate which factors operating in a given social situation are the basic, important ones. Systems of beliefs are like theories; they may be right or wrong in the sense that they predict—correctly or incorrectly—what will happen.

---

[9] Ibid., p. 249.

[10] Arthur H. Miller, Warren E. Miller, Alden S. Raine, Thad A. Brown, "A Majority Party in Disarray: Policy Polarization in the 1972 Election." Paper delivered at the 1973 meeting of the American Political Science Association, New Orleans. This paper appeared in revised form in the *American Political Science Review*, vol. 70 (September 1976), pp. 753–78.

[11] Campbell et al., *The American Voter*, p. 250.

[12] See Robert Putnam, *The Beliefs of Politicians* (New Haven: Yale University Press, 1973), pp. 4–7; John D. Steinbruner, *The Cybernetic Theory of Decision* (Princeton, N.J.: Princeton University Press, 1974).

A conservative Republican probably holds such ideas as that privately owned corporations, markets, and independent groups tend to provide more effective means of attaining social ends than does government; that government efforts to equalize the distribution of economic goods probably do more harm than good in most instances; that society is better off if individuals of superior character are allowed to pursue wealth and other goals freely without government intervention; and that this will lead to a redistribution of wealth to those persons who deserve it. These and other related beliefs—theories about society—can be linked in a reasonably consistent pattern of ideas that we would call a conservative Republican system of beliefs. Similarly, we might describe the belief system of a liberal Democrat, who would surely hold different beliefs about the efficacy of government action in attaining social goals, the consequences of taxing business and giving to the poor, and so forth. The conservative will infer from his system of beliefs that taxes should be decreased and that food-stamp programs should be cut back. The liberal will infer from his system that food stamps—and the taxes to pay for them as well—should be increased.

In other words, the issue-oriented participant may infer positions on political issues from a system of beliefs. Such a system saves mental energy. If a person determinedly attempted to approach every single political issue inductively, he would be forced to spend his entire waking existence studying politics. No one could approach even two or three political issues—for example, the question of the number of nuclear power plants that should be constructed and the question of the laws that ought to be adopted to regulate the financing of political campaigns—without spending his entire life on them if he were to proceed on the basis of pure induction. Inability to cope with reality lies in both too much induction and too little.

But there are other systems of political beliefs than those that we call liberal Democrat and conservative Republican which have evolved in the last generation. From our observations of public interest groups, I conclude that most leaders and most followers of such groups believe in something I will call civic balance, to give it a deliberately bloodless name. Later I observe that beliefs concerning civic balance help the leaders of public interest groups decide what positions to take on complex energy issues, such as the question of deregulation of natural gas.

The elements of the civic-balance system of beliefs are these: the political system is seen as complex, fragmented into numerous areas of policy; such policy areas are often controlled by unrepresentative elites, however, who act to further their own special interests to the detriment of the interests of the great majority of the public; such public interests frequently go unrepresented in policy making, either because public interests, such as those of consumers, are inherently hard to organize, or oligopolies or bureaucracies, acting singly or in combination, defeat those agents working "in the public interest"; hence there is a need for citizens to organize into groups and participate in the political process in order to balance the power of the special interests.

Among other things, the theory of civic balance is a rudimentary theory of representation. This system of beliefs implies that widely shared interests are not adequately represented in many of the numerous policy systems which, added together, form our government. The theory of civic balance implies that unless citizens form new institutions for representation, American government will have an elitist character, in that economic, political, and bureaucratic leaders will control public policy for their own benefit, rather than for the benefit of the public.

Civic-balance theory permeates the political communications issued by many public interest groups. To illustrate what I mean by civic-balance beliefs, let us examine recent mass mailings sent from Common Cause and from Ralph Nader. Such mailings represent a major organizational investment. They are written with great care. I am confident that they state actual beliefs of John Gardner and of Ralph Nader. While the statements below were written with the intent to persuade, they are similar to numerous other public statements of Mr. Gardner and Mr. Nader.

Let us turn to a recent Common Cause mailing: "Common Cause: Modern Americans Fighting for Principles as Old as the Republic." It is an elegant ten-page brochure, designed to fit inside a standard business envelope. Between 1 and 10 million copies will be mailed, depending on its success in obtaining new members. The text begins with a statement of the theme of special interests versus the "people's interests" and the need for citizens' organizations to attain a more representative form of government:

> Our nation's founders did not leave us a completed task . . . they left us a beginning. It is our obligation to define and dislodge the modern obstacles to the fulfillment of our founding principles. Because, as visionary as they were, our founders could not have foreseen *how dominant special interests would become* through the accumulation of wealth and power, and through skillful secret dealings with government officials.
>
> In the face of this, people like you and me—people who reject apathy and cynicism—must join forces to fight for

open and accountable government. How? By joining Common Cause and supporting our efforts to create direct and immediate changes in the political system. [Emphasis added; ellipsis points in original; paragraphing adjusted.]

The next section of the text faces a full-page picture of a founding father, Benjamin Rush, "Treasurer of the U.S. Mint," who is quoted as having said: "The influence of wealth at elections is irresistible." The text is a particularly direct statement of the civic-balance belief system:

> THANKS TO COMMON CAUSE, THE INFLUENCE OF WEALTH IN ELECTIONS IS SHRINKING. In Benjamin Rush's day, money could influence elections. A century and a half later, it could dominate them. By lavishing contributions on candidates, well heeled *special interests* came to exercise decisive leverage over the outcome of elections. Matched against this enormous power, the principle of fair elections often proved a feeble challenger.
>
> That is, until Common Cause changed the odds by strengthening the *people's interest* through election reforms. Our members threw themselves behind the cause of campaign finance reform. Our highly skilled lobbyists *pressured* Congress. Our volunteers monitored campaigns throughout the country. And our staff disclosed the cozy relationships between candidates and *special interest* contributors. [Emphasis added; paragraphing adjusted.]

It might be noted that John Gardner has become uneasy over the connotations of the term *the public interest* and substitutes *the people's interest*, as does Nader in a passage quoted below. It is also noteworthy that Gardner refers to Common Cause as having "pressured" Congress, indicating the expressly political orientation of Common Cause, in contrast to the apolitical quality of some early twentieth-century Progressive reformers, who advocated "scientific management" in "the public interest."[13]

Civic-balance theory is further expounded on the next page of text, where it is applied to Congress:

> Congress was never intended to be a bulwark against *the people's interests*. But a self-perpetuating system of favors and rewards caused its committee structure to become just that. Committee chairmen who favored *special interests* were richly rewarded with campaign contributions. With better financing than their challengers, they repeatedly won

---

[13] Grant McConnell, *Private Power and American Democracy* (New York: Alfred A. Knopf, 1966), pp. 11–50.

re-election. In turn, they used the power of their seniority to side with *the special interests*. Common Cause was determined to dismantle this structure by toppling its two strongest pillars: seniority and secrecy. [Emphasis added; paragraphing adjusted.]

The following mailing on behalf of Nader's Public Citizen organization was sent in 1974. Its opening litany of complaints uses the "special interests versus people's interests" type of language. The implication is that special interest rule is at least partly to blame for the social ills cited in the letter.

From: Ralph Nader

Dear Friend:

Recently, a young woman asked me whether there was anything bigger than the Watergate scandal in Washington. I replied: "Yes, the 'citizen gap.'"

A "citizen gap" opens when business or governmental abuses prevail without citizens doing anything about them.

Just about everybody has experienced "citizen gap."

—Have you ever felt there was a wall around City Hall?

—Have you wondered why Congress so often responds to the monied interests instead of the peoples' interest?

—Have you grumbled about high taxes for the many and large loopholes for the favored corporations and millionaires?

—Have you had that helpless feeling against inflation, especially fast rising food, energy, medical and housing prices?

—Have you gotten sick over the poisonous pollution of our priceless air, water and soil which sustain human life and health?

—Have you felt unable to do anything at all about shoddy consumer goods and companies who don't respond to your legitimate complaints?

—Do you wonder how our country could have so many problems when it has such wealth, talent and know-how to overcome them?

—Do you feel an uneasy frustration over the growing concentration and secretiveness of economic and political power?

If you identify with any of these reactions, you're experiencing "citizen gap."

The letter continues by pointing out that contributing to Public Citizen can help eliminate "that gap." Language reflecting civic-balance assumptions continues to be used:

> Our tax reform attorneys provided the decisive leadership in 1972 in blocking $400 million in *special interest tax bills* about to be sneaked through Congress without even a public hearing. This year, they have worked for the abolition of corporate tax loopholes and the improvement of the IRS procedures for small taxpayers. [Emphasis added.]

These extracts should be sufficient to demonstrate that the civic-balance belief system is an important part of Nader's view of the world.

I offer the hypothesis that holding civic-balance beliefs predisposes those with some college education to support public interest groups. Since the number of the college educated is increasing, the subset of the educated holding civic-balance beliefs has also been increasing. Furthermore, there is evidence that the *proportion* of those holding civic-balance beliefs is also increasing.

The Growth of Civic Skepticism. During the last decade, the decline in popular trust of our national political institutions, as indicated by survey research, is quite shocking. Increasing skepticism extends not only to national institutions in general but to such specific institutions as the Congress and the political parties.[14] After inspecting the data in Tables 2 and 3, one may very well conclude, in the words of the old popular song, "something's gotta give." These and other data indicate an extraordinary decline in the level of trust in national political institutions as expressed to survey research interviewers. But of course what people *say* when interviewed and what they actually *do* is another matter. For example, skeptical responses do not necessarily imply that the respondent will drop out of politics. On the contrary, he might become active in support of a candidate who expresses a skeptical point of view and who appears to be different from the usual breed of "untrustworthy" politicians.

Another type of action suitable for citizens skeptical of existing political institutions is to support a public interest group. Many must have done so, although their number constitutes only a small fraction of the total number of skeptics. But this growth of skepticism can be

---

[14] See Jack Dennis, "Trends in Support for the American Party System," *British Journal of Political Science,* vol. 5 (April 1975), pp. 187–230; Arthur H. Miller, "Political Issues and Trust in Government: 1964–1970"; Jack Citrin, "Comment"; and Miller, "Rejoinder," *American Political Science Review,* vol. 63 (September 1974), pp. 951–1001.

Table 2

DECLINE OF POPULAR TRUST IN SOCIAL INSTITUTIONS:
HARRIS SURVEY RESPONSES, 1966–1974

Q. I want to read you some things some people have told us they have felt from time to time. Do you tend to feel or not feel—	**Percentage of Voters Agreeing**			
	1966	1972	1973	1974
The rich get richer and the poor get poorer?	45	68	76	79
Special interests get more from the government than the people do?	n.a.	n.a.	74	78
The tax laws are written to help the rich, not the average man?	n.a.	74	74	75
The people running the country don't really care what happens to you?	26	50	55	63
Most elective officials are in politics for all they personally can get out of it for themselves?	n.a.	n.a.	60	62
What you think doesn't count much anymore?	37	53	61	60
You feel left out of things going on around you?	9	25	29	32

n.a. Not available.
Source: "Public Disaffection at Record High," *The Harris Survey*, released 27 June 1974. Cited by Jack Dennis, "Trends in Support for the American Party System," *British Journal of Political Science*, vol. 5 (April 1975), p. 227.

seen as another factor inducing the recent growth and influence of public interest groups.

The link between skepticism and public interest participation can be seen in the activity of these groups. Again we can turn to their mass mailings; they are full of statements intended to persuade the "civic skeptics" that public interest participation is worthwhile. This did not happen by accident. All such mass mailings are pretested. This is a cardinal rule of direct-mailing practice. A proposed mass mailing is first sent to a small group similar in composition to the larger group that is the eventual target. If the rate of response is adequate, then larger amounts of money are invested to send out the successful mailing. Thus, we know that if the League of Women Voters, Common Cause, and Ralph Nader stress the message of skepticism and the possibilities of public interest action, their experience indicates that those with skeptical political attitudes constitute an important pool of

Table 3
DECLINE OF POPULAR TRUST IN GOVERNMENT:
SURVEY RESPONSES, 1964–1970
(percent)

Q. How much of the time do you think you can *trust* the government in Washington to do what is right—*just about always, most of the time,* or *only some of the time?*

Response	1964	1966	1968	1970
Always	14.0	17.0	7.5	6.4
Most of the time	62.0	48.0	53.4	47.1
Only some of the time[a]	22.0	31.0	37.0	44.2
Don't know	2.0	4.0[b]	2.1	2.3
Total	100.0	100.0	100.0	100.0
(N)[c]	(4658)	(1291)	(1557)	(1514)

Q. Would you say the government is pretty much run by *a few big interests* looking out for themselves or that it is run for the *benefit of all* the people?

Response	1964	1966	1968	1970
For benefit of all	64.0	53.0	51.8	40.6
Few big interests[a]	29.0	34.0	39.2	49.6
Other; depends; both checked	4.0	6.0	4.6	5.0
Don't know	3.0	7.0	4.3	4.8
Total	100.0	100.0	100.0	100.0

Q. Do you think that people in the government waste *a lot* of the money we pay in taxes, waste *some* of it or *don't waste very much of it?*[d]

Response	1964	1966	1968	1970
Not much	6.5	. . .	4.2	3.7
Some	44.5	. . .	33.1	26.1
A lot[a]	46.3	. . .	57.4	68.7
Don't know; not ascertained	2.7	. . .	5.3	1.5
Total	100.0		100.0	100.0

Q. Do you feel that almost all of the people running the government are smart people who usually *know what they are doing,* or do you think that quite a few of them *don't seem to know what they are doing?*[d]

Response	1964	1966	1968	1970
Know what they're doing	68.2	. . .	56.2	51.2
Don't know what they're doing[a]	27.4	. . .	36.1	44.1
Other; depends	1.9	. . .	1.8	2.3
Don't know; not ascertained	2.5	. . .	5.9	2.4
Total	100.0		100.0	100.0

14

Q. Do you think that *quite a few* of the people running the government are a little crooked, that *not very many* are, or that *hardly any* of them are crooked at all?[d]

Response	1964	1966	1968	1970
Hardly any	18.2	. . .	18.4	15.9
Not many	48.4	. . .	49.3	48.8
Quite a lot[a]	28.0	. . .	24.8	31.0
Don't know; not ascertained	5.4	. . .	7.5	4.3
Total	100.0		100.0	100.0

[a] Indicates reponse interpreted as "cynical."
[b] Includes 1 percent coded "It depends."
[c] The sample size for each of the years applies to all five items. The 1964 *N* is weighted.
[d] These items were not included in the 1966 election study interview schedule.
Source: Arthur H. Miller, "Political Issues and Trust in Government: 1964–1970," *American Political Science Review*, vol. 68 (September 1974), p. 953. The data were compiled from national sample surveys of eligible voters conducted by the University of Michigan Survey Research Center. Used by permission of the American Political Science Association.

potential members. If this were not the case, they would invest their money in other types of messages.

The reader may have noticed that statements in public interest group mailings closely resemble the statements used by survey researchers to measure "distrust of government," "political cynicism," and "political alienation," to mention terms sometimes used in this context.[15] For example, compare:

Special interests get more from the government than the people do.

Harris Poll

Would you say the government is pretty much run by a few big interests looking out for themselves or that it is run for the benefit of all the people?

Michigan Poll

Have you wondered why Congress so often responds to the monied interests instead of the peoples' interest?

Ralph Nader

. . . our founders could not have foreseen how dominant special interests would become through the accumulation of wealth and power. . . .

Common Cause

[15] See, for example, Dennis, "Support for the American Party System"; Miller, "Trust in Government."

Or we can compare:

The people running the country don't really care what happens to you.

Harris Poll

Have you ever felt there was a wall around City Hall?

Ralph Nader

... there is neither the custom nor the pretense of accountability in many Executive agencies, departments and commissions. Yet they routinely establish both policy and practice, unhampered by the will of the people or their elected officials.

Common Cause

In a mass mailing for recruitment, dated October 1974, Ruth C. Clusen, president of the League of Women Voters, started her letter with explicit references to the extent of skepticism and allying the league with such skeptics:

> Dear Fellow Citizen:
>   I think you'll agree that the last few years have left a lot of Americans feeling disillusioned about their government and public institutions. Pollsters report, in fact, that the current mood of disenchantment is so pervasive that a majority of every major segment of the populace is turned off by politics, and questions the fairness of our economic system and the role accorded the individual in our society. According to a Harris poll taken earlier this year, a significant 63 percent believe "The people running the country don't really care what happens to you." And 60 percent said, "What you think doesn't count much anymore."
>   We at the League of Women Voters and League of Women Voters Education Fund hope that you're not only disillusioned, but disturbed and concerned enough to want to do something. WE ARE!

Another expression of skepticism is found in the following excerpts from a mass mailing sent by the Natural Resources Defense Council in June 1974:

> At this very moment, gigantic monsters are tearing away at some of the most picturesque and fertile land in our country ... they are engaged in one of the most ruinous assaults ever unleashed on the environment: strip mining. ... Because years of efforts to legislate the abolition of stripping have ended in abject failure, the Natural Resources Defense Council took the Tennessee Valley Authority to court last year over its failure to comply with the National Environmental

16

Policy Act. . . . Rarely has there been a better opportunity or a more urgent need to safeguard our vanishing heritage.

It is important to note that this letter expresses disillusionment in the possibility of congressional action to deal with the "monster" of strip mining. Nor will government agencies, such as the Tennessee Valley Authority (TVA), necessarily follow the law. The letter clearly implies that laws often go unenforced.

We term such ideas *civic skepticism*. The civic skeptic is a liberal or an independent who once thought that government was capable of dealing with important social problems that concerned him. In this, he differed from the conservative skeptic, who never believed that government could command the means to end poverty, solve the problems of the cities, end racism, and so forth. The civic skeptic, on the other hand, once believed that Kennedy, Johnson, Humphrey, Rockefeller, Lindsay, and the rest could institute great public programs that could make significant headway against such major social problems. But now he is a skeptic. He no longer believes that government, as it is constituted at present, can accomplish great social reforms. Further, the civic skeptic believes that government is frequently unrepresentative—it is often in the hands of the special interests. But this type of person still retains a bit of optimism. Perhaps, he thinks, government and politics can change their quality. Perhaps new institutions can be formed that will be more representative and can help mitigate social evils. Such an optimistic skeptic may join a public interest group. Certainly the communications from such groups stress the themes of political skepticism and of optimism that new institutions can be formed.

From the historical point of view, it is important not to confuse the attitudes held by the Progressives and by the New Dealers toward government and politics with the civic skepticism that prevails today. The Progressives believed that they could establish government agencies and regulatory commissions that would administer progressive reforms in a neutral, scientific manner in the public interest. They believed that it is possible to take politics out of administration.[16] Until the time of Lyndon Johnson's presidency, New Dealers and liberals had a different idea. They thought that great social reforms could be achieved through the establishment of a powerful, political executive branch, unified and directed by a powerful President, and supported by a similarly minded Congress and political party. The leaders of the public interest groups of today have still another idea, however.

They are for reform, but reform through ad hoc coalitions. In the

---

[16] For a criticism of such views, see Dwight Waldo, *The Administrative State* (New York: Ronald Press, 1948).

view of the new civic reformers, pressure must be put on the President, Congress, and the executive branch from outside if reform laws are to be implemented. True, these reformers press for the creation of new agencies—such as Nader's demand for a consumer protection agency or Common Cause's insistence that a powerful federal elections commission be established. But neither Mr. Nader nor Mr. Gardner imagines that such new agencies, designed to implement public interest reforms, will be effective unless they are supported by political power from the outside, including backing from public interest groups.[17]

Reform laws, and agencies to implement them, are backed by ad hoc coalitions, limited as to subject matter and in time. Typically one of the larger public interest groups will take the lead in lobbying for a bill. Nader, for example, will take the lead in calling for creation of a consumer protection agency, Common Cause will take the lead in support of legislation to regulate campaign financing, and so forth. (The public interest position on energy matters is yet relatively disorganized, so no particular group exercises leadership in that area. This is the role to which Americans for Energy Independence aspires.) The public interest group leader will work with congressmen who exercise leadership with respect to a particular issue (Nader with Senator Ribicoff on auto safety, Common Cause with Congressmen Morris Udall and John Anderson on campaign-finance legislation). The congressmen and the public interest group then form links with journalists, concerned pressure groups, officials in the executive branch, and individual citizens. In sum, an ad hoc coalition is formed around the public interest issue—the public interest group that is leading in support of the issue, other public interest groups, congressmen, members of the executive branch, other interest groups, journalists, and individual citizens. Such a coalition may be formed around the goal of getting a bill passed by Congress, or it may be formed to ensure enforcement of some reform legislation, a much more difficult task.

Another aspect of action through outside pressure and ad hoc coalitions is public interest litigation.[18] This tactic is now familiar to politically aware Americans, but its use became widespread only in 1966, with the emergence of Nader as a national figure. Government agencies are sued for failure to enforce existing legislation, injunctions are obtained against public works projects pending the satisfactory

---

[17] Interview with John W. Gardner, October 1975. Also see Charles McCarry, *Citizen Nader* (New York: Saturday Review Press, 1972), pp. 75–96.
[18] See Joseph L. Sax, *Defending the Environment* (New York: Alfred A. Knopf, 1971).

18

submission of environmental impact statements, and so forth. Public interest litigation is a tactic viewed as effective by most persons who follow politics, although the degree of effectiveness is a matter of dispute: Are such lawsuits only delaying tactics, or are they a new institution that has been added to our political system? This question cannot be answered here. But public interest litigation is much more effective when it is conducted by well-organized, influential public interest groups than it is when suits are initiated by individual citizens who happen to be aggrieved by some practice affecting consumers, the environment, or the electoral system. Lawsuits are expensive and require considerable legal and technical skills, which are best furnished by an established organization. The defense by Common Cause of the 1974 campaign reform act has cost about $150,000 so far; so much documentation was necessary that it had to be wheeled into court in a shopping cart. Public interest lawsuits frequently are a type of ad hoc coalition activity; they have specific goals and are often the result of the efforts of several supporting groups.

Thus skepticism can bring social advances. The public interest leaders of the 1970s are much more skeptical about government than their forebears of the Progressive Era or the New Deal. The new civic reformers do not believe in boards of independent experts or in a powerful executive branch. They look to ad hoc coalitions to get legislation passed and to similar coalitions or to public interest lawsuits to get such legislation enforced. In this respect they have made a contribution to the American reform tradition.[19]

In summary, the growth of skepticism towards government institutions was a factor related to the development of public interest groups in the early 1970s. Leaders of such groups frequently display a belief that we term *civic skepticism*—the idea that government frequently does not represent public interests but that citizens' organizations can do something to rectify this imbalance. Expressions of skepticism in mass mailings have proved to be an effective way for public interest groups to attract members. The new civic skepticism has provided an advance in reform tactics—the ad hoc political coalition sup-

---

[19] I do not mean that all activities of public interest groups proceed from the assumptions of civic skepticism and ad hoc coalitions. Some smaller or local groups may still express Progressive or New Deal attitudes toward government. Further, sophisticated public interest groups may avoid facing the problem that great efforts are often necessary to get reform legislation enforced. Thus, People's Lobby and California Common Cause were surprised at the amount of effort required to get the famous Proposition 9, a lobbying and campaign-reform initiative, administered in a way they consider to be favorable. Similarly, Common Cause is discovering that guarding the powers of the Federal Election Commission, which is attempting to regulate congressional and presidential politics, is more difficult than it anticipated.

plemented by the public interest lawsuit. Now let us turn to the other four factors related to the recent growth of public interest groups. We can describe these more briefly.

Leadership. It is hard to imagine the public interest movement in its present form without the figures of Ralph Nader and John Gardner. Their activities have constituted an important stimulus for the appearance of influential public interest lobbies.

Nader has both charisma and technical skills. The ascetic, dedicated prophet of the public interest is the object of widespread admiration. Thousands of young persons desire to emulate him. Those who work for Nader organizations in Washington are expected to take on aspects of the Nader personality—to work long hours for subsistence pay and to conduct themselves with moral rectitude. On the other hand, Nader has technical skill. His long hours of study have made him well informed, although perhaps in the sense of an advocate arguing one side of a case. He has the journalist's instinct and skill for spotting news and conveying it dramatically to the public.

Such abilities enable Nader to raise $2 million a year for his cluster of about fifteen organizations in Washington. He has assembled a group of fifty to seventy-five talented persons who work full time in Washington for the various causes that he advocates. Within reasonable limits, Nader can publicize any issue and put it on the national political agenda. These are impressive accomplishments. But his most impressive accomplishment is his contribution to the practice of ad hoc coalition politics in the public interest, which puts the new civic reformers a step ahead of the Progressive and the New Deal liberals. Working with friendly congressmen, journalists, tipsters within the executive branch, dedicated staffers, and volunteers, Nader has been able to place issues before Congress and has thus been prominent in the effort to protect the consumer and to regulate big business. He has demonstrated thereby the possibilities for effective coalition politics in the interests of the public, using techniques of data gathering, publicity, lobbying, and lawsuits.

The founding of Common Cause in the summer of 1970 was an impressive feat of leadership on the part of John Gardner. While not well known to the public at large, Gardner was highly regarded by a large section of the upper middle class and by the agenda setters and policy makers of Washington and New York. His following among the educated had been gained with the help of two best-sellers, *Excellence* and *Self-Renewal*,[20] which contained observations about self-

[20] John W. Gardner, *Excellence* (New York: Harper & Row, 1961); *Self-Renewal* (New York: Harper & Row, 1964).

fulfillment in modern society and about ways in which a creative in-
dividualism might prevent "organizational dry-rot" in contemporary
American society. Gardner gained his following among the policy elite
through his activity as an innovator in educational policy while he was
president of the Carnegie Foundation. As secretary of health, education, and welfare (1965–68), he impressed most observers with his
performance in that hot seat of American government, which generally
lowers the reputation of those who sit in it.

Contrary to the opinion of most sophisticated observers, Gardner
decided that it would be possible to establish a mass-membership,
citizens' lobbying effort. He was right. Common Cause was an immediate success. One reason for its success was a heavy reliance, in the
newspaper advertisements and mass mailings that were the basis of
membership recruitment, on Gardner's reputation for moral leadership
and political skill. (Nader was one of those who thought a mass-
membership solicitation wouldn't work, and thus the Common Cause
effort preceded the Public Citizen effort by about a year.)

Since 1970, Common Cause has flourished, with membership
ranging from 200,000 to 320,000 and budgets ranging from $4 million
to $6 million. Such success has been due in large part to Gardner's
sagacious leadership. Thus, internal conflict was minimized and political impact was maximized by the emphasis of Common Cause on
government-reform issues. With the help of his right-hand men, Jack
Conway and David Cohen, Gardner assembled a group of highly
skilled persons for the national staff, which included lobbyists, public
relations experts, direct-mail specialists, political organizers, writers,
computer operators, and policy analysts. Gardner's influence permeates
the entire structure of Common Cause. It is hard for the staff of
Common Cause to imagine their organization without Gardner, and
thus when he hinted publicly in early 1975 that he might retire in
1978, many were genuinely shocked.

Technology. Certain advances in technology are one of the reasons
that national public interest lobbies achieved influence only in 1970,
rather than, say, 1950. Communications technology is particularly important to the existence of public interest groups, because the interests
they represent are typically widespread but not immediately perceived
by those whom they affect. Such issues as the environment, consumer
protection, good government, and now energy frequently require explanation, and even dramatization, before people can be aroused to
action in regard to them.

News programs on television are important in the development of
support for public interest issues. Nader is highly telegenic, and the

issues he supports thus get wide publicity. The environmentalist movement was strengthened by televised news. Few persons have seen a strip mine, an oil spill, Alaska, or a nuclear power plant, but these things can be made objects of immediate perception by means of television journalism. It is thus easier now for environmentalists to attract supporters beyond their basic constituency of conservationists, hikers, and sportsmen than it would have been in the 1940s.

As noted earlier, computer-based mass-mailing techniques are used to gain members and contributions for public interest organizations. Common Cause got about 80 percent of its 275,000 members by means of direct-mail promotion; Consumers Union nearly tripled its membership by using the same techniques; Nader's Public Citizen is purely a mail operation; the American Civil Liberties Union has greatly expanded its membership by the use of direct-mailing techniques. Common Cause has sent out about 40 million solicitations for membership; this organization could not have existed in its present form if it had had to depend on hand typing of address labels and hand filing of address lists.

The development of relatively cheap, reliable, and quick (direct distance dialing) telephone communications gives a new advantage to national political organizations. Common Cause in particular uses five Wide Area Telephone System (WATS) lines, thereby renting five long-distance lines at a flat monthly rate. A basic part of the lobbying organization of Common Cause is the link between about 250 volunteers in the national headquarters and a representative in each of the 350 congressional districts in which Common Cause maintains a local organization. Thus when the national office wants to pressure Congress on an issue, it can make immediate contact with its local members by telephone. The local members are organized into telephone networks (one person calls seven), so that when Washington calls the district, letters and telegrams are soon on their way. Computer technology helps with the telephoning. Every month the membership of Common Cause is analyzed by congressional districts, and fresh lists of members are sent to local organizations, so that the local leaders know who has joined, who has withdrawn, who has moved out or in, and what their addresses and phone numbers are.[21]

Prosperity. This factor requires little explanation. Fifteen-dollar membership contributions are frequently among the first items to be cut from the budgets of middle-class families striving to maintain their standards of living during inflation. The successful attraction of wide-

---

[21] Statements about Common Cause are based upon the author's ongoing study of that organization.

spread contributions by Common Cause (1970) and Nader's Public Citizen (1971), as well as the expansion of Consumers Union, occurred during a time of relative economic prosperity. But 1974 and 1975 were years of budget cuts for most public interest groups. It would have been much more difficult to launch a mass-membership public interest group in 1975 than it was in 1970–71.

Initial Success Brings More Success. First let us examine success in the sense of gaining mass support. Well-publicized legal victories by environmentalists in 1969 meant that donors to such groups as the Sierra Club, the Natural Resources Defense Council, or to any of thousands of ad hoc local efforts could expect an effective use of their money. By the time of Nader's mass mailing in behalf of Public Citizen in 1971, he had gained a reputation for effectiveness in putting issues before Congress, and thus, again, a donor could expect that his money would be used effectively. About 125,000 persons joined Common Cause before that group had achieved its initial successes in opposing the SST and in helping to organize antiwar congressmen in the House to get a vote of overall approval or disapproval of the war effort. (Speakers McCormack and Albert had blocked such a vote for six years.) Many of these persons might have dropped their membership however—about 65 percent renewed—if they had not had some assurance from the leaders of Common Cause that their lobbying was effective. This assurance was given in mail solicitations and in newsletters by quoting public statements of Senators Kennedy, Scott, Mondale, and others complimenting the Common Cause lobby in opposition to the SST.

Another way in which success brings more success is illustrated by the fact that a reputation for power and effectiveness in the past helps one gain power in the present.[22] Politicians are more readily persuaded by lobbyists who have some reputation for "clout." It is my impression, on the basis of twenty interviews with members of the House on a tangential matter, that most congressmen do not want to be quoted publicly in criticism of Nader, Common Cause, or the League of Women Voters. These groups are evidently seen as capable of causing at least minor difficulties for a congressman. The great surge in support for environmentalism and ecology in early 1969 meant that for two or three years most politicians felt that they had to give the impression of support for environmental questions or else

---

[22] Richard E. Neustadt, *Presidential Power* (New York: John Wiley & Sons, 1960); Reputation for power, however, a power base, should not be confused with power itself: Andrew S. McFarland, *Power and Leadership in Pluralist Systems* (Stanford, Cal.: Stanford University Press, 1969), pp. 5–6.

be criticized by future political opponents, letter writers, demonstrators, local newspaper and TV editors, ministers, high-school and college teachers, scientists, and others.

But, of course, countervailing factors will check the success of public interest groups. After a few years, the public became aware of the costs of environmentalism in increased prices and increasing uncertainty of employment. Nader overextended himself in 1971–72 in his massive study of Congress, out of which a monograph on each congressman was produced. These evaluations appeared to have little effect on the 1972 congressional elections however. One chairman of a House committee reported to me that this failing effort reduced Nader's reputation for clout, since it showed that he could not readily influence congressional elections on a mass basis.

Finally, success may undercut itself, particularly in times of economic trouble. Some donors might expect that others would begin to contribute to a successful public interest organization, thereby relieving the first group of responsibility for continuing their contributions. The view "they don't need my money" can hurt public interest groups.

This is not presented as an exhaustive or definitive treatment of the rise of public interest groups in the last few years. For some reason, however, there is no published social-scientific treatment of the recent rise of public interest groups. I hope that this section will serve as an adequate beginning in the understanding of this important phenomenon in American politics of the present day.

2

PUBLIC INTEREST LOBBIES AND "THE LOGIC OF COLLECTIVE ACTION"

One of the purposes of this monograph is to initiate an understanding of the recent phenomenon of public interest groups. Further, it is useful to discuss these groups within an intellectual context, rather than relying upon the argumentation of political debate, for, indeed, public interest groups are now politically controversial because they have power. In this section I lay out the context in which I view such groups—their functioning as a means by which widespread but diffuse interests can be represented in a pluralist democracy.

I examine the idea of civic balance in relation to the theoretical work of political economist Mancur Olson, Jr. We find that the civic-balance system of beliefs sometimes portrays reality. Specific policy systems can get out of balance, because certain types of "public interests" are particularly hard to organize and thus are not readily expressed in a pluralistic struggle for influence among organized interest groups. This is not to paint public interest groups with unalloyed virtue. Such groups do not always express public interests; special interests sometimes promote public interests; sometimes in a policy situation there are several conflicting public interests. These questions are complicated, but they are at the heart of many issues facing our society today.

The Political Debate about Public Interest Groups

Let us here briefly note the political debate about public interest groups. Scores of persons from different social sectors have expressed their views to me regarding the nature of public interest groups; I have encountered other views in the media. Critics and defenders of public interest groups regularly accuse one another of hypocrisy, selfishness,

LIBRARY
OF
MOUNT ST. MARY'S
COLLEGE
EMMITSBURG, MARYLAND

stupidity, elitism, and other vices. It is possible to conduct these arguments on more of an intellectual level however.

Conservatives criticize public interest groups for masking liberal ideology in a public interest disguise. They think that public interest groups do not understand the workings of a market economy and that the proposals of public interest groups tend to cause additional economic problems, such as inflation, loss of jobs, and higher taxes. Proponents of public interest groups, in turn, argue that defenders of free enterprise do not understand the realities of an economy tending toward oligopoly. The public interest movement, its defenders argue, is actually restoring competition and free markets through its advocacy of open government, antitrust measures, licensing of corporations, campaign reform, and so forth. Of course counterarguments are possible—the virtues of large productive units, the usual failure of antitrust action, and so forth—which can be followed by counter counterarguments.

Many liberal Democrats also criticize the public interest movement. Some liberals charge the public interest groups with diverting the political agenda away from the "Great Society" issues—racial inequality, the condition of the cities, poverty, the redistribution of wealth, and so on. Liberals and conservatives alike criticize public interest groups for representing group interests, as opposed to public interests. The platforms of public interest groups—environment, consumerism, open-government reforms, and the like—are said to refer to the special interests of middle-class elements. In the face of such criticism, public interest proponents may reply that the poor, the racial minorities, and the working classes suffer proportionately more from special interest "ripoffs" than do persons with high incomes—pollution is worse in the city, for example, prices are higher and quality is poorer in the ghetto, and lunch-bucket meals are not subject to tax deductions as business expenses. They argue that it is fitting for higher-income elements to tax themselves voluntarily by contributing to public interest groups for the sake of improving life for all elements of society.

Critics charge that public interest groups are insensitive to the need for economic growth—something that is very important to the public at large—and to the need for jobs, when public works projects are blocked. Defenders of public interest groups reply that America is moving into an era of slower growth because of worldwide scarcity of resources and that we must begin the adjustment now. Such persons would argue that jobs are not eliminated by environmental measures and others that they support, but are only transferred: if a steel mill is

26

shut down in Indiana, for example, a factory making antipollutant devices may at the same time be expanding and creating new jobs.

Critics charge that public interest groups frequently make decisions on the basis of inadequate information—especially in situations which are highly technical. Certainly energy policy raises questions that are technical and complex. The revised Rasmussen report, dealing with the safety of water-cooled nuclear reactors, is about 1,800 pages long and could be the basis of a yearlong seminar in the field of engineering.[1] How can citizens deal with such technical matters? Public interest groups reply by pointing to whatever technical expertise they can field, and by pointing out that while experts do know the most about their specialties, they may be among the most biased of persons when it comes to judging the value of their specialized products to the public at large. Persons who have committed themselves to a profession or a specialty naturally come to believe in the vital importance of their field and its technical apparatus. Society must somehow gain the benefits of expert technical advice while remaining skeptical of the specialist's bias concerning the social usefulness of his specialty. Public interest groups want to participate in decision making that is related to technical questions.

I hope that the public will examine the merits of the various positions in the debates between supporters and critics of public interest groups. As noted earlier, a problem of representative government is fundamental to evaluating the role of public interest groups—the question of representing interests that are widespread but difficult to organize in a pluralist democracy. The work of political economist Mancur Olson, Jr. is basic to the understanding of this question.

Mancur Olson, Jr.: "The Logic of Collective Action"

The fundamental question posed in this work is: Do people form interest groups when they have some common interest in influencing public policy?[2] After applying economic analysis to the question, Olson comes to the conclusion that large groups frequently will *not* become organized, while small groups, on the other hand, usually will organize. Olson's analysis leads to a perspective that is parallel to

---

[1] U.S. Nuclear Regulatory Commission, *Reactor Safety Study: An Assessment of Accident Risks in U.S. Commercial Nuclear Power Plants*, WASH-1400 (NUREG-75/014), October 1975. See also the appendices to the main report.

[2] Mancur Olson, Jr., *The Logic of Collective Action* (Cambridge: Harvard University Press, 1965). A revised edition, issued in 1971, has the same pagination, but an appendix has been added.

Michels's law of oligarchy:[3] Organized, narrowly based elites tend to defeat unorganized majority interests. Olson has described in a new way how particular interests will rule to the detriment of widely shared, or "public," interests. He emphasizes reasons that large publics do not organize and is only secondarily interested in the description and tactics of special interest rule.

Olson begins his book with these observations:

> It is often taken for granted, at least where economic objectives are involved, that groups of individuals with common interests usually attempt to further those common interests. . . . The view that groups act to serve their interests presumably is based upon the assumption that the individuals in groups act out of self-interest. . . . But it is *not* in fact true that the idea that groups will act in their self-interests follows logically from the premise of rational and self-interested behavior. . . . Indeed, unless the number of individuals in a group is quite small, or unless there is coercion or some other special device to make individuals act in their common interest, *rational, self-interested individuals will not act to achieve their common or group interests.*[4]

Why won't groups, especially large ones, form? Because, in Olson's scheme, there is no incentive for the individual to organize such a group or to join it, if it should already have been organized. This is particularly true in the case of large publics that have widely shared economic interests of secondary importance to individuals—such as consumers, for example. Consequently, because there is insufficient incentive for individuals to form interest groups in such situations, these groups will not form, and important interests will not be represented in public policy.

There are two aspects to this problem of organizing large publics. The first aspect is the costs of organization. If a large number of people is involved, it is not worthwhile for an individual, or several individuals, to form an organization and lead it into political battle, for the fruits of success will be worth less than the costs in time and money of organizing. For example, many months of full-time political effort would be required for some desired change in a consumer product to be brought about. From the standpoint of economic analysis, we cannot expect the rational individual to follow such a course of action. A second aspect is the free-rider problem. In a situation in which a substantial number of persons is involved, if an interest group has

---

[3] See Robert Michels, *Political Parties*, trans. Eden and Cedar Paul (New York: Collier Books, 1962).

[4] Olson, *Collective Action*, pp. 1–2.

already been formed and is pursuing some beneficial public policy or acquiring some public goods, persons who are not members can usually obtain the benefit whether or not they contribute to the organization that has secured it. It is not rational for them to pay for the goods when they can obtain them free anyway. The greater the number of nonpaying beneficiaries, however, the more difficult it is to maintain the group and to obtain the benefit in question. The economic result is the production of a suboptimal quantity of the good; the political result is that an interest group or lobby will have political resources that do not correspond to its popularity. Eventually the existence of a large number of free-riders will lead to the dissolution of the organization if it cannot attract sufficient contributions to support the achievement of its goals. Educational television stations that rely upon voluntary contributions to stay on the air exemplify this situation. One can watch the station without paying, but if too great a share of the audience does so, the station cannot stay on the air. Until the 1970s, national consumer lobbies got very little support from the general public, who enjoyed the benefits of the successes (however limited) of such lobbies but did not contribute to the lobbies in large enough numbers to make them truly influential.[5] Of course, such discussions of organizational costs and free-riders presume the existence of an economic cost-benefit analysis. Individuals are seen as calculating the costs in time and money of various alternatives and then pursuing the least costly alternative to a particular goal. Actually, economic motivations are often secondary to other types of motivations. Most readers would regard such a view of human motivation as applying to a rather limited scope of human activity, albeit a significant one.

The Logic of Collective Action is subtitled "Public Goods and the Theory of Groups." To simplify somewhat, a "public good" is one which, by its very nature, if it is available to one member of some public, must be available to everyone. If there is an educational television program in a given community, it is there for everyone (presuming that everyone has access to a receiver). Olson's situations are such that a public good or "collective good" is provided for everyone in some group, and thus individuals can become free-riders and get their share of the collective benefit without having worked for it. In Olson's words:

> The concept of public goods is one of the oldest and most important ideas in the study of public finance. A common, collective, or public good is here defined as any good such that, if any person X_i in a group $X_1, \ldots X_i, \ldots X_n$ consumes

5 See Mark V. Nadel, *The Politics of Consumer Protection* (Indianapolis: Bobbs-Merrill Company, 1971).

it, it cannot feasibly be withheld from the others in that group. In other words, those who do not purchase or pay for any of the public or collective good cannot be excluded or kept from sharing in the consumption of that good, as they can where noncollective goods are concerned.[6]

In other words, when a public or collective good is produced (possibly as a result of action taken by a government or the efforts of a lobby), then the free-rider problem emerges, because it is infeasible to exclude nonpaying beneficiaries from the enjoyment of the particular good.

We should note that Olson's use of public goods terminology is confusing. In the literature on public finance, the term *public goods* has an areal association and tends to be identified with the activities of the state, as opposed to the firm. Classic public goods are national defense, a system of criminal justice, and a clean and healthy physical environment. Such goods are produced by the state for everyone within some geographical area. Olson, however, extends this accepted usage of *public goods* and, aware that he is doing so, tends to substitute the term *collective goods* for public goods in the book.

> Students of public finance have, however, neglected the fact that the achievement of any common goal or the satisfaction of any common interest means that a public or collective good has been provided for the group. The very fact that a goal or purpose is common to a group means that no one in the group is excluded from the benefit or satisfaction brought about by its achievement.[7]

Thus groups produce "collective goods" for their members, and thus interest groups are subject to the free-rider problem. The point is a good one, but this confusing usage of *public goods* has already produced another confusion among some political scientists. Thus, one cannot cite Olson's usage and define a public interest lobby as one that produces "public goods." Olson himself notes that a tariff could be "a public good to the industry that sought it" and that "the removal of the tariff could be a public good to those who consumed the industry's product."[8] But if one adopts the definition just noted, both a special interest lobby and a consumers' lobby would be "public interest" lobbies, because both would be seeking "public goods," in Olson's usage. This is really quite confusing, and thus the definition of a public interest lobby cannot simply follow from Olson's usage of the term *public goods*.

---

[6] Olson, *Collective Action*, pp. 14–15.

[7] Ibid., p. 15.

[8] Ibid., p. 15, footnote.

Writing at a time when the idea of a public interest was in disrepute among political scientists, Olson avoids using the term itself. But throughout his book, he is concerned with the problems referred to by others in special interest versus public interest terminology. Thus, Olson's book ends on a pessimistic note:

> The existence of large unorganized groups with common interests is therefore quite consistent with the basic argument of this study. But the large unorganized groups not only provide evidence for the basic argument of this study: they also suffer if it is true.[9]

And, not only are such widespread "common interests" hard to organize, they are also opposed by well-organized special interest lobbies.

> The consumers are at least as numerous as any other groups in the society, but they have no organization to countervail the power of organized or monopolistic producers. . . .
> There are multitudes with an interest in peace, but they have no lobby to match those of the "special interests" that may on occasion have an interest in war. . . .
> There are vast numbers who have a common interest in preventing inflation and depression, but they have no organization to express that interest.[10]

> The taxpayers are a vast group with an obvious common interest, but in an important sense they have yet to obtain representation.[11]

> Often a relatively small group or industry will win a tariff, or a tax loophole, at the expense of millions of consumers or taxpayers in spite of the ostensible rule of the majority.[12]

In such cases, other writers would refer to "public interests."[13]

But we have not yet reached the depth of pessimistic implications inherent in *The Logic of Collective Action*. Thus not only will "common interests" fail of organization, their opponents, the "special

---

[9] Ibid., p. 167.

[10] Ibid., p. 166.

[11] Ibid., pp. 165–66.

[12] Ibid., p. 144.

[13] See, for example, Emmette S. Redford, *Ideal and Practice in Public Administration* (Birmingham: University of Alabama Press, 1953), Chapter 5; Grant McConnell, *Private Power and American Democracy* (New York: Alfred A. Knopf, 1966), Chapter 10.

interests," often can organize with ease to influence public policy.[14] Olson tends to identify such special interests with particular business lobbies, but bureaucratic groups, alliances of governmental units, or various types of coalitions among such actors could constitute an organizable special interest. Olson makes a tripartite distinction in the size of groups and their propensity to organize. He refers to very small groups, in which at least one actor has an incentive to produce the collective good, as privileged groups, in which the collective good will be surely produced. Then there are intermediate groups, in which the propensity to organize is indeterminate, and the latent groups, which are so large that they cannot organize without the inducements of coercion or of especially created goods to attract members (insurance for members of the Farm Bureau, for example). An intermediate group is similar to what the economists call "oligopoly."

> In the intermediate or oligopoly-sized groups, where two or more members must act simultaneously before a collective good can be obtained, there must be at least tacit coordination or organization.[15]

> An "intermediate" group is a group in which no single member gets a share of the benefit sufficient to give him an incentive to provide the good himself, but which does not have so many members that no one member will notice whether any other member is or is not helping to provide the collective good. In such a group a collective good may, or equally well may not, be obtained, but no collective good may ever be obtained without some group coordination or organization.[16]

Olson makes the point that organizable intermediate groups will frequently defeat the *un*organizable latent groups.

> Although in relatively small groups ("privileged" or "intermediate" groups) individuals may voluntarily organize to achieve their common objectives, this is not true in large or latent groups.[17]

> Since relatively small groups will frequently be able voluntarily to organize and act in support of their common interest, and since large groups normally will not be able to do so, the outcome of the political struggle among the

---

[14] Olson, *Collective Action*, pp. 144–45. Olson uses the term *special interests* frequently, but he always puts this term within quotation marks.

[15] Ibid., p. 46.

[16] Ibid., p. 50.

[17] Ibid., pp. 126–27.

various groups in society will not be symmetrical. Practical politicians and journalists have long understood that small "special interest" groups, the "vested interests," have disproportionate power. The somewhat too colorful and tendentious language with which the men of affairs make this point should not blind the scholar to the important element of truth that it contains. The small oligopolistic industry seeking a tariff or a tax loophole will sometimes attain its objective even if the vast majority of the population loses as a result. The smaller groups—the privileged and intermediate groups—can often defeat the large groups—the latent groups which are normally supposed to prevail in a democracy.[18]

Thus, according to Olson, the tendency for minority rule over particular issues is not just a problem of democracy, it is a frequent occurrence in the contemporary American political system. This is largely the result of the fact that business is divisible into sectors, most of which are oligopolistic and therefore easily organizable for the purpose of influencing public policy.

The number and power of the lobbying organizations representing American business is indeed surprising in a democracy operating according to the majority. . . . The high degree of organization of business interests, and the power of these business interests, must be due in large part to the fact that the business community is divided into a series of (generally oligopolistic) "industries," each of which contains only a fairly small number of firms. Because the number of firms in each industry is often no more than would comprise an "intermediate" group, it follows that these industries will normally be small enough to organize voluntarily to provide themselves with an active lobby.[19]

Although he stresses the political power of oligopoly, Olson clearly disagrees with those who argue that America is dominated by a business-oriented power elite. "Although particular industries normally have disproportionate power on questions of particular importance to themselves, it does not follow that the business community has disproportionate power when dealing with broad questions of national concern."[20] This is because the general business associations—the National Association of Manufacturers and the U.S. Chamber of Commerce—are also subject to the free-rider problem and hence must rely upon the

---

[18] Ibid., pp. 127–28.
[19] Ibid., pp. 142–43. Original italics omitted.
[20] Ibid., p. 145.

donations of a small minority of the business community. "The business community *as a whole* is not a small privileged or intermediate group—it is definitely a large, latent group. As a result it has the same problems of organization as the other segments of society."[21] The point is an interesting one, illustrating in a novel way the limitations of the NAM and the U.S. Chamber of Commerce. When the interests of business as a whole are called into question in the United States, however, business can expect to be well represented, even if its general associations have limited influence.

Thus Olson provides a fairly rigorous argument for the contention that American democracy is seriously flawed by the control of particular issue areas by special interest elites to the detriment of common interests, which are difficult to organize.

Criticisms of "The Logic of Collective Action"

In general Olson views his work as a contribution, based upon economic thought, to the general theory of society, comparable in generality, if not in scope, to the work of the most renowned academic writers on this topic.[22] As such, Olson's work is naturally subject to criticism at the higher levels of theoretical generality. An obvious criticism is that political man is not economic man and that persons have various altruistic or emotional motivations which lead them to act in ways that are different from those that time/money cost-benefit calculations would imply. (Most people vote, for instance, even though individual votes seldom make much difference.) Brian Barry has argued that Olson's work lends itself to tautological formulations: If a latent group is organized, there must be a "selective incentive" present, and the definition of selective incentives is so general that one could hardly ever fail to find one.[23] (A selective incentive is some benefit that is distributed to the organized members of a latent group, making it profitable for individuals to join the group. A selective incentive could be anything from reduced rates on insurance policies to social prestige to the prospect of going to heaven rather than to hell.) Various writers have pointed out that political entrepreneurs may appear who will find it personally profitable to provide the collective good to the latent group and that under these circumstances, individuals may find it

---

[21] Ibid., pp. 145–46.

[22] Ibid., appendix to revised edition.

[23] Brian M. Barry, *Sociologists, Economists and Democracy* (London: Collier-Macmillan Publishers, 1970), pp. 33–37.

worthwhile to contribute toward the provision of the collective good.[24]

In my view, all these criticisms have merit, but I believe Olson to have great value for his understanding of the dynamics of certain types of power relations. Emphasis on Olson's general theoretical shortcomings may obscure his contribution to the study of political power and representation.

The study of power is a study of relationships. Understanding political power involves the understanding of who wields power over whom. Thus Olson's contribution to the study of practical politics is his observation that small groups frequently defeat large groups. One need not agree with everything Olson has to say about economic motivation, collective goods, and free-riders in order to agree with him when he says,

> since relatively small groups will frequently be able voluntarily to organize and act in support of their common interests, and since large groups normally will not be able to do so, the outcome of the political struggle among the various groups in society will not be symmetrical. . . . The small groups—the privileged and intermediate groups—can often defeat the large groups—the latent groups—which are normally supposed to prevail in a democracy.[25]

Here Olson's analysis seems quite relevant, particularly in areas in which economic considerations are important—the regulation of business in the interest of the consumer, protection of the environment, and so forth. The costs of organization and communication and the free-rider problems usually are less for one or a few corporations in their lobbying efforts, as opposed to such costs for a vast majority who have economic interests in conflict with those of the lobby. Olson here focuses on a cost relationship—the public as a whole could be organized only at a high cost to oppose a small group of corporations or bureaucrats, which could be organized at much lower cost. In such a relationship, the small group could be expected to win, but such a victory might be against "the public interest" (an interest of a large public). This phenomenon may occur with respect to a single issue or within a single sector of the total economy.

Another criticism of *The Logic of Collective Action* is that politicians will seek to please important latent groups in order to win

[24] Norman Frohlich, Joe Oppenheimer, and Oran Young, *Political Leadership and Collective Goods* (Princeton: Princeton University Press, 1971); Robert Salisbury, "An Exchange Theory of Interest Groups," *Midwest Journal of Political Science*, vol. 13 (February 1969), pp. 1–32.

[25] Olson, *Collective Action*, pp. 127–28.

votes. This point is made in a review article by Richard Wagner;[26] it is similar to a general line of argument in Robert A. Dahl's *Who Governs?*, a prominent work in contemporary political science.[27] (In his *After the Revolution?*, Dahl implicitly concedes that elections cannot control the policies of large corporations to a satisfactory extent.[28]) Wagner's point is correct to some degree, but as Olson notes in response: "The most casual observation of modern democracies, and particularly of the special interest legislation they have passed, makes clear that it matters a good deal whether a group is organized or not."[29] Thus presidential, congressional, or gubernatorial aspirants will frequently adopt public interest rhetoric in campaigning for office. Consumer and environmentalist causes will be supported; tax equity will be affirmed; inflation-producing special interest legislation will be denounced. But this does *not* imply that legislation to these ends will be passed or that such laws will be enforced if they are passed. In passing legislation, and in enforcing it, Olson's small-group versus large-group dynamic applies, particularly in situations in which a few economic units are in opposition to diffuse public interests.

Olson provides a justification for the need for public interest groups. Those who believe in representative democracy and pluralism must admit that the problem of organizing widespread latent publics poses problems for their political philosophy. I believe that public interest groups are needed to fulfill the function of representing latent publics in contemporary America. This does not necessarily imply, however, that the stands of public interest groups always correspond to the interests of widespread publics. Furthermore, other agencies can represent widespread latent interests. Certainly there is an incentive for politicians to do so. Depending on who is right on policy issues related to energy, some corporations might be representing public interests. (It may be in the interests of a great majority to move in the direction of deregulation of natural gas, for example.)

Liberals and independents may find Olson's work more readily acceptable than will conservatives. I have heard conservatives offer this type of argument on a number of occasions, however, with respect to preventing inflation and keeping down government expenditures, the power of the federal bureaucracy, and the power of labor unions.

---

[26] Richard Wagner, "Pressure Groups and Political Entrepreneurs: A Review Article," *Papers on Non-Market Decision Making, 1966*, pp. 161–70.

[27] Robert A. Dahl, *Who Governs?* (New Haven: Yale University Press, 1961), pp. 163–65, 218–20.

[28] Robert A. Dahl, *After the Revolution?* (New Haven: Yale University Press, 1970), pp. 115–40.

[29] Olson, *Collective Action*, rev. ed., p. 174.

For example, conservatives typically agree that logrolling among special interests produces excessively high governmental expenditures, which contributes to inflation, which is detrimental to the interests of the public at large. No conservatively oriented public interest group is now influential at the national level, although taxpayers' unions seem to be influential in some states. I expect that if a liberal Democrat were to be elected President, however, with Democrats in control of Congress at the same time, there would be a move to organize a conservative public interest group emphasizing such questions as the control of federal expenditures and the prerogatives of public employees.

Public Interests and Complex Policy Systems

In considering Olson's contribution to the understanding of the problems of representing widespread but diffuse interests (hereafter referred to as the diffuse-interests problem), it is important to avoid the error of "public interest singularity." In other words, Olson leaves one with the impression that in specific policy situations, latent groups are often opposed to special interests in a one-versus-one manner. In most policy situations we want to analyze, however, including most energy matters, there are *several different* public interests and several different particular interests involved in the same situation. In most of the interesting policy situations, we have public interest *A*, public interest *B*, and so forth, and *not* one single public interest involved in the policy situation. While it may be possible to define *a* public interest in *a* situation with some clarity, such a perspective is usually misleading.

Economist Edward J. Mitchell provides us with an illustration of this kind of complexity in an energy policy situation, which is diagramed in Table 4. Professor Mitchell introduces the diagram as follows:

> Perhaps the most crucial energy issue to come before the Congress is the President's bill to deregulate the wellhead price of new contract natural gas to be sold in interstate commerce. It is assumed here that the natural gas producing industry is competitive, and that the principal initial impact of deregulation would be to raise the price of new gas. . . . I will attempt here to indicate some of the winners and losers if such a bill were to pass, but it must be recognized that this is only a rough speculation.[30]

[30] Edward J. Mitchell, "Research on Energy Policy-Making," in Hans H. Landsberg et al., *Energy and the Social Sciences: An Examination of Research Needs* (Washington, D.C.: Resources for the Future, 1974), p. 586.

Table 4
GAINERS AND LOSERS FROM DEREGULATION OF NATURAL GAS PRICES

Gainers	Losers
Owners of natural gas resources	Natural gas consumers with assured supplies of domestic gas for many years[a]
Oil and coal consumers[a]	
Owners of resources complementary to gas in consuming states	Some employees of the Federal Power Commission
Producing state governments and taxpayers[a]	Intrastate pipelines
	Owners of resources complementary to gas in the producing states
Suppliers of drilling equipment	Shipyards building LNG ships (and their employees)
Suppliers of oil in regions where gas would no longer be competitive with oil (New England, for example)	Oil producers (highly correlated with gas producers)
Breathers of air in consuming states[a]	Coal producers
	Builders of synthetic gas plants
Federal Treasury and taxpayers[a]	Breathers of air in producing states[a]
Natural gas consumers who would otherwise be cut off[a]	Suppliers of oil in regions where gas has been short (e.g., middle Atlantic states)
Interstate pipelines	Propane suppliers
Consumers of imported items[a] (due to higher exchange value of the dollar)	Natural gas consumers in producing states[a]
	Oil exporting nations
U.S. importers (other than oil and gas)	U.S. exporters

[a] Latent group.
Source: Edward J. Mitchell, "Research on Energy Policy-Making," in Hans H. Landsberg et al., *Energy and the Social Sciences: An Examination of Research Needs* (Washington, D.C.: Resources for the Future, 1974), p. 587.

In the table, latent groups are indicated in Olson's sense of interests that are widespread but difficult to organize. These latent interests are in the consumer, environmentalist, and taxpayer categories. While the exact number of them is not important for our purposes, it is interesting to see that there are nine latent interest groups involved—six on one side and three on the other. Also involved are seventeen particular interests—that is, the financial interests of particular industries or groups. Such complex policy systems are typical in the politics of energy. Indeed, such complexity is typical in most policy-making situations in present-day America.

The interests marked latent are those which have problems in organizing. To the extent that politicians and judges do not speak for these interests, they need representation by public interest groups. We think that there is such a need with respect to most aspects of public policy, certainly with respect to energy policy.

It is interesting to note that public interest groups concerned with this issue have been active only on the side of regulation and not on the side of deregulation. I think this to be a result of the civic-balance system of beliefs. Public interest groups at present usually see themselves as balancing the power of corporate and bureaucratic power groups, and such groups have been powerful in pressing for deregulation. Public interest groups inclined to favor deregulation (some conservationists privately are sympathetic to this side) do not become active because, in view of their limited resources, they decide to let the oil companies handle the matter. Further, their taking such a position would anger part of their constituency—contributors, staff, journalists, and the like—who hold to the civic-balance theory. In other words, these constituents see public interest groups as having the function of opposing corporate interests that throw the weight of public policy in the direction of special interests. They would vigorously criticize a public interest group for joining the main body of corporate lobbyists on the gas deregulation issue.

I caution the reader that one cannot easily quantify the interests involved in a complex policy system such as that expressed in Mitchell's diagram. There is no basis for concluding a priori, for example, that because there are six public interests on the side of deregulation and only three on the other side, the overall interest of the public is on the side with six. Different persons will give different weights to the values involved, and there is no objective way to quantify or to aggregate such values.

By now the major point of this section should be clear: Widespread, difficult-to-organize, diffuse interests of latent groups sometimes lack representation in complex policy-making systems. Public interest groups provide a useful approach to the representation of such diffuse interests. But this does not mean that a stand of a public interest group represents *the* public interest and provides an ethically superior solution to a policy question. Typically there are *several* latent groups or public interests that need to be represented, and these may be arrayed on both, or on several, sides of a policy question. Somehow the government ought to give attention to the various public interests and special interests concerned in a situation, and somehow an equitable policy should be made.

It goes beyond the scope of this work to state the characteristics of a decision-making system in which the interests of all those affected by a decision, such as the twenty-six different interests listed by Mitchell in the natural gas deregulation issue, would be balanced equitably. Describing the way in which such decisions *are* made by government, and theorizing about how they *ought* to be made, is the heart of the study of public administration in a democracy. A leader in the field, Emmette S. Redford, referred to this type of question as "the central quandary of democratic theory" in his *Democracy in the Administrative State.* He asks: "How can distributed, low-quantity interests of the many and high-quantity interests of the few in particular policy confrontations be mediated? . . . in a pluralistic society the democratic morality runs full force into the problem of a balance on representation of interests of varied quantities."[31]

Nor can we settle the question of how public interests, in Olson's sense, ought to be represented in governmental processes. We can make two basic points, though. First, when such public interests are eventually organized, their representatives need to have significant access to governmental decision makers, particularly high-ranking officials in executive agencies. Second, public interest groups need to have some clout—at least enough political support to ensure frequent and respectful attention from decision makers. A civil servant, influential in the field of energy policy, told an interviewer: "Sure, I meet with environment groups—all the time. But I don't pay any attention to what they say!" Public interest groups need to have enough members and supporters—politicians, journalists, government officials, and others—that if they are ignored in some situation, they can get a hearing by appealing to the public at large.

On Defining "Public Interest Lobby"

Having followed the topic for five years, I can state with confidence that no one in the country today can give a really good, analytical definition of *public interest lobby.*[32] I can offer a usage definition of the term that will serve the purposes of this study, however.

By "usage definition" I mean defining the term according to the way it is used among politicians in Washington. In present-day political usage, a *public interest lobby* is one that seeks to represent general interests or those of the whole public; does *not* chiefly represent some specific economic interest; and is *not* a lobby in one of the following

---

[31] Emmette S. Redford, *Democracy in the Administrative State* (New York: Oxford University Press, 1969), p. 22.

[32] For an introductory treatment of this question, see Virginia Held, *The Public Interest and Individual Interests* (New York: Basic Books, 1970).

traditional categories: religion, ethnic groups, race, regional interests, women's rights, avocational groups, and perhaps others.[33]

By this definition, Common Cause, the Nader organizations, the Consumer Federation of America, and Consumers Union are public interest lobbies. In the last generation, the League of Women Voters has been primarily a good-government group, and it has been only secondarily a lobby for the rights of women. The Sierra Club at one time may have been a sportsmen's group, but certainly in the last decade it has devoted its lobbying efforts to conservation and protection of the environment. The Americans for Energy Independence are an interesting borderline group. It is not yet clear whether this organization will become a federation of several groups serving particular economic interests or one which seeks to represent the interests of a broader public.

A group may be called a public interest lobby without invariably lobbying for widespread economic interests or good government. In my opinion, lobbying simultaneously for a moratorium on the construction of nuclear power plants *and* for strict environmental controls on the production of oil and coal (which would preclude the development of Wyoming-Montana coal), for example, is not for the benefit of the public at large. Similarly, the reader may very well conclude that many of the stands of public interest groups described herein do not represent widespread interests of the public at large.

Furthermore, while public interest lobbies do not always represent public interests, "special interest" groups, such as corporations or bureaucracies, may frequently represent diffuse interests, in Olson's sense. For example, if one believes that the gradual deregulation of natural gas would benefit a preponderant majority of the public, then it follows that corporate lobbying for deregulation represents public interests. Or, to take a less controversial example, in the spring of 1976 a lobby of shoestore owners represented consumer interests in working to defeat a proposal to raise the tariff on imported shoes substantially.

There is another complication in discussing public interest lobbies. Some say that public interest groups, particularly environmentalist groups, are pursuing special interests. Take the suit of the Friends of

---

[33] The ambiguity of this list reflects ambiguities in the usage of the term *public interest group* among politicians. Peace groups, animal-protection lobbies, various "cause" groups (for example, pro- and anti-abortion groups and the Women's Christian Temperance Union) are puzzling categories. Some persons would refer to some of them as public interest groups; others would not. Such differences cannot be resolved without an extended debate on the matter by political scientists, or the emergence of a second Wittgenstein to solve the conceptual puzzles involved. See Hanna Fenichel Pitkin, *Wittgenstein and Justice* (Berkeley: University of California Press, 1972).

the Earth, the Environmental Defense Fund, and others to block the construction of the oil pipeline to Alaska, for example. Since the majority of Alaskans wanted the pipeline and since production of oil in Alaska is in the economic interests of the "lower forty-eight," one can say that the suit of the environmentalists represented the special interests of consumers of undeveloped wilderness. One could offer a similar argument concerning the development of the Wyoming-Montana coal fields, although here it appears that the majority of local inhabitants opposes development. Ninety-eight percent of Americans will never see this region of proposed strip mining in the Northern Plains. One can readily argue that Northern Plains coal mining corresponds to the interests of the general public (particularly if a technology of "scrubbing" soot particles out of the emissions of coal-burning electric plants is developed). Environmentalist groups opposing Northern Plains coal would be regarded by some as representing special interests.

However, the terminology of public interest versus special interests, particularly as it is used in reference to environmentalist groups, can be misleading. Conflicts over environmental issues are frequently a matter of conflicting moral ideals, rather than of conflicting cost-benefit analyses. Most supporters of the Sierra Club, for example, will never visit Alaska or northern Wyoming. It is somewhat misleading to say that a Sierra Club supporter has an *economic* interest in preserving wilderness in these areas. Instead, the motivation of the typical environmentalist appears to be moral and ideological. I would say that the committed environmentalist is a believer in a secular natural law. He believes in a natural law in the sense that he believes that man should treat nature with respect. This secular natural law implies that mankind's technologies should harmonize with nature, rather than disrupt it, intrude upon it, or change it drastically. It follows that the committed environmentalist, when he regards some technological project as particularly violative of this ideal of natural law, will not cease opposing the project, even if he is confronted with an overwhelming amount of cost-benefit analysis demonstrating that it is beneficial to the public at large. And to the committed environmentalist, ecological natural law will even take precedence over the civic-balance system of beliefs, which is shared by most environmental activists. Thus, the environmentalist ordinarily sees himself as protecting public interests against depradation of the environment by special interests. But when confronted with some economic cost-benefit analysis that shows him to represent the special interests of a minority, the chances are that the environmentalist will not reverse his position and support some technological intrusion upon nature, because protecting nature is the primary value and civic balance is secondary.

Thus, public interest groups do not always represent public interests; special interest groups sometimes represent public interests; environmentalists, using public interest rhetoric, frequently are defending a type of natural law. The term *public interest lobby* masks considerable confusion. I will continue to use this term throughout the rest of the volume because it is the one commonly used, but a better term would be *citizens' lobby*. If we used that term we could avoid the tangle of arguing about who *really* represents public interests. A citizens' lobby could be said to be mistaken in its judgment that some position is representative of public interests without generating so much of an emotional charge as one does in saying that a public interest lobby is not really representing public interests. For example, one might believe that the Sierra Club was representing public interests yesterday and the day before, but that today the Sierra Club is taking a special interest position. But if one should say publicly that the Sierra Club is representing special interests and not public interests today, one would seem to be extremely critical, if not downright hostile. It would sound as if one were unmasking the Sierra Club as some egregious type of fraud, rather than merely stating a simple, temporary disagreement.

I have treated the rise of public interest lobbies in recent years. I then turned to an examination of Olson's idea of latent groups, to the complexity of policy systems, and to the idea that public interest groups do not necessarily represent public interests. I hope that these ideas will have put public interest lobbies in a useful perspective. Now let us turn to their decision-making practices on energy matters.

3
ENERGY POSITIONS AND ORGANIZATIONAL STRUCTURE

Perhaps a score of public interest groups have some lobbying effectiveness with respect to national energy policy. Unfortunately, within the limited scope of such a study as this, all of these groups cannot be treated, nor can a history of the influence of public interest lobbies on energy policy be offered.

My chief interest is in the mass-membership public interest groups, which is the reason for my having done field research on Common Cause. I have included in this study certain other groups with large memberships: the League of Women Voters (140,000 members), the Sierra Club (125,000 memberships, or 153,000 members), and Consumers Union (1.8 million subscribers eligible to become voting members).[1] Along with Common Cause, Ralph Nader's organizations, taken together, are the most influential public interest lobbies, and for that reason I have included them within this study. As a federation of about 200 groups, the Consumer Federation of America can claim to speak for a wide spectrum of the public, and I therefore became curious about its energy task force. Finally, Americans for Energy Independence has a fresh approach to organizing, although it may yet collapse or become a more usual type of economic lobby.

The stands of these groups on energy are analyzed according to their organizational stance in this area of policy (initiator of policies versus aggregation of various policies for example). Organizational role is in turn related to a group's characteristics, such as structure and resources.

---

[1] The Sierra Club has joint memberships for spouses, and thus they make a distinction between memberships and members. The figures for Common Cause, the League of Women Voters, and subscribers to *Consumer Reports* are "memberships" in this terminology. For example, the figure of 275,000 Common Cause "memberships" counts a "Mr. and Mrs." only once.

I do not intend to demean public interest groups by relating their energy positions to organizational characteristics. Indeed, I have indicated in the preceding chapter that such groups are needed to represent difficult-to-organize, widespread economic interests. But the staff and supporters of public interest groups are human like the rest of us. How do they, then, select those particular public interests which they endorse from the more numerous set of public interests existing in regard to some policy? The organizational characteristics of public interest groups limit such choices. Given an array of public interests which might be served, a reasonable person will not choose to pursue some goal which would destroy his organization when there is an alternative public interest goal which would enhance the group. (We are presupposing the existence of complex policy systems, usually having several different public interests, which may lie on both sides of a question.)

Five Positions on Energy Policy

The organizational characteristics and decision making of public interest lobbies can be related to five positions with respect to energy policy, each implying a distinct way of dealing with energy problems in the future. These are (1) development and independence, (2) a mixture of regulation and market mechanisms, (3) the same as number two, but with emphasis on developing coal, (4) low energy growth, and (5) development of an informed public opinion on energy. I shall describe these positions briefly, then turn to an exposition of the stands of the various groups.

Development and Independence. This is my term for the overall outlook of the Ford administration and its supporters in the field of energy policy. This outlook stresses the necessity for independence of imported oil and the consequent need to develop all the major present sources of energy—oil, gas, coal, and nuclear. A high value is set upon conservation of energy, but it is not assumed that life styles need be changed greatly in the next ten years. Such moderate changes as speed limits of fifty-five miles an hour, energy conservation codes for federal buildings, and so forth are advocated.

In this position, environmental values must give way to development in a number of important situations: drilling for offshore oil is supported; the Udall strip-mining control bill is opposed;[2] the con-

---

[2] See *Congressional Quarterly Almanac*, vol. 30 (1974), pp. 759–73.

struction of several hundred more nuclear power plants is supported; strip mining, shale oil development, and conversion of coal to gas in western areas of low rainfall are also supported.

Supporters of development give nuclear energy the benefit of the doubt. They want to see nuclear electricity-generating plants increase from the present 58 in operation and about 64 under construction to perhaps 650 plants by the turn of the century. They support the development of the breeder reactor (which would create more plutonium fuel than is put into it) and expensive plants to reprocess plant wastes into useful fuel. The developers think that the benefits of increased electric power are worth the risks of possible release of radioactive elements into the community, the problem of the disposal of deadly radioactive wastes, and the consequences of the release of large volumes of heated water into streams in the vicinity of nuclear power plants. In 1974–76, however, increasing costs of plant construction, of uranium, and of enriching uranium have suddenly called into question the economic advantage of nuclear plants over coal-fired electricity-generating plants. Thus a new factor in supporting nuclear power is the desire to help an industry that has an uncertain economic future.[3] But principled supporters of free enterprise ought to consider whether federal expenditures of billions of dollars for the breeder reactor and other substantial governmental aid to the nuclear power industry are in fact consistent with a belief in the economic efficiency of unregulated markets.

Supporters of development want to lessen government regulation of the energy industry and want the federal government to deregulate the price of "old oil" and of natural gas shipped in interstate markets. They support free enterprise and see no need to break up the larger oil companies or to establish a federal oil and gas corporation.

The Mixed-Market Policy. By this I mean a position which includes more government regulation than the first, but which would still use market mechanisms to a considerable extent. This is the Common Cause approach, in contrast to that of the Ford administration (development) or to that of the Nader and environmentalist groups (more regulation).

The mixed-market policy includes a major emphasis on conservation, involving significant (but not radical) changes in life styles. Advocates of this position would accept government deregulation of

---

[3] See, for example, "Why Atomic Power Dims Today," *Business Week*, November 17, 1975, pp. 98–106. Also see David Burnham, "Hope for Cheap Power from Atom Is Fading," *New York Times*, November 16, 1975, p. 1.

petroleum and natural gas, partly because the resulting price rises are seen as the most effective way to reduce consumption. Supporters of this position are neither particularly hostile nor particularly friendly to the oil industry. If higher oil and gas prices were to lead to rapid rises in profits, such profits would be taxed away, according to the advocates of the mixed market.

The development of nuclear power is being phased out of this position. Supporters of the mixed market are neither so optimistic about nuclear power as the developers nor are they so critical as the environmentalists. This position now calls for a moratorium on the licensing of the construction of nuclear plants beyond the 120 already licensed. Advocates of the mixed market were not particularly critical of the development of nuclear power until recently, however, when a wave of criticism hit the nuclear power industry in 1974–76. Consequently, if the nuclear power industry is able to demonstrate the safety of its operations in the context of the need to get more energy from somewhere, advocates of the mixed market, who appear to be genuinely open to changing their minds, could probably accept the construction of more nuclear power plants. In line with the acceptance of the market mechanism as a good means of regulation, advocates of the mixed market regard the Price-Anderson Act (federal subsidies for insurance against disastrous incursions of radioactivity into the environment) as a special financial favor which should be repealed.

Policy developers adhering to the mixed-market outlook are just now realizing that if one supports the moratorium on construction of nuclear power plants, and if one does not consider radical changes in life styles to be politically feasible, then one must greatly increase the production of coal for the generation of power. The stance of this group is considered as a third position (see below).

The market or price mechanism does not necessarily imply private ownership of all firms. One can believe in the relative efficacy of pricing as a means of economic regulation, as opposed to the imposition of regulations by the government, and yet advocate that one or more of the competing firms be publicly owned. Thus, the advocates of the mixed market, while favorably disposed toward the gradual deregulation of oil and gas, are also in favor of the idea of establishing a federally owned gas and oil company to compete with privately owned corporations. One justification offered for this position is that the oil industry is becoming increasingly public, because oil production is increasingly the subject of decisions vital to the future of our society. Detailed information about production of oil and gas is needed for public decision making about energy, yet such information cannot, and should not, be obtained from private corporations by coercion. A federal corporation, it is argued, can provide us with a yardstick by which to judge the operations of private corporations in providing us with energy.

Advocates of the mixed market are not very much interested so far in the idea of breaking up the large oil companies by antitrust action. The idea of divesting the oil companies of their holdings in the coal- and uranium-mining sectors appeals to such persons, however.

The Common Cause variant of the mixed-market position places great stress on "openness" in decision making by the government with respect to energy. Common Cause is thus searching for ways to make an outside, public presence felt in the making of decisions by such agencies as the Federal Energy Administration and the agencies of the Interior Department issuing coal and oil permits. Common Cause regards increased citizen presence in energy agencies of the executive branch as an example of healthy competition, an idea in accord with the general mixed-market outlook.

The Mixed Market Plus Coal. I think that this mixed-market approach will become the most popular alternative to the idea of development among the public at large. The Nader-environmentalist low-energy-growth position is too radical to gain widespread acceptance. The oil and gas price-regulation policies popular with liberals in Congress will become discredited, I think, as production lags. A platform of encouraging competition, reducing the power of special interests in federal energy agencies, and ending subsidies, which also accepts the need for considerable government action (excess profits taxes, a government oil company, active sponsorship of research into alternative sources of energy, and so forth), seems destined to be popular. It is already popular to criticize both big government and big business and to call for an end to regulation and subsidies, as does Governor Edmund G. Brown, Jr., of California.

But the mixed-market position has a flaw. If a nuclear moratorium is advocated, it will apparently be necessary to substitute coal-fired electric power, since we do not want to import still more oil from OPEC producers. But mixed-market advocates are just now beginning to examine the problems associated with a possible major increase in coal production in the next decade. The cheapest available coal which could be readily brought to production lies close to the surface in Montana, North Dakota, and northern Wyoming. The environmental questions posed by the strip mining of such coal will constitute a dilemma for mixed-market advocates. Another environmental dilemma will be posed by the need to use large amounts of water in the possible construction of massive coal-to-gas conversion plants in these same relatively arid western regions. Furthermore, pollution and lung cancer can follow the release of exhaust fumes from coal-burning power plants, although a technology of "scrubbing" such fumes is now being developed.

The mixed-market approach needs to contain a position on coal mining if it is to be convincing. Advocates of this approach are just beginning to work out such a position. They may find, however, that there is no way to increase coal production rapidly unless strip-mining methods that are harmful to the environment are used.

Low Energy Growth. Here we are referring to citizens' lobbies that are critical of development of the present major sources of energy. Such groups enthusiastically advocate a nuclear moratorium (in contrast to the reluctant advocacy of the moratorium by Common Cause and other mixed-market advocates). In fact, judging from the overall slant of their criticism of nuclear power, Nader and the environmentalists would evidently like to shut down the nuclear power plants now in operation.

Dedicated as these citizens' advocates are to environmental preservation, it is hard to see how they would permit significant increases in production of oil, gas, or coal in their projection of the future. Instead, low-growth advocates tend to emphasize the possibilities for solar power. This performs a useful public service, since the political process needs vocal lobbyists for the development of this alternative source of energy. In my opinion, solar power will not be developed in the next fifteen years to an extent which would take up the slack from a 120-plant ceiling on nuclear power plants, no increase in domestic production of oil and gas, and only moderate increases in domestic production of coal.

The combination of a nuclear moratorium, severe restrictions on offshore drilling, tough strip-mining controls or the abolition of strip mining altogether, opposition to oil shale development and coal-to-gas conversion, and (theoretically) continued government regulation to bring about lower petroleum and natural gas prices would result in a lessening of supply, a clear-cut environmental preservation policy, and a great need for far-reaching energy-conservation measures. Actually, even though Nader and some environmentalist groups oppose deregulation of oil and gas pricing, in practice they may assume that deregulation will come to pass. Thus, John Abbotts of Nader's Public Interest Research Group writes: "Continuing higher prices will tend to drive the growth in energy demand towards the same rates as population growth."[4] Presumably such "continuing higher prices" would reflect a gradual deregulation policy (although oil prices might be held below OPEC levels).

The "alternative scenarios" of Abbotts presume that coal production will yield 21 quadrillion BTU by 1985, up from 12 quadrillion in 1974, and that domestic oil will yield 32 quadrillion BTU in 1985, up from 22 quadrillion in 1974. Many observers would deny that such increases are possible in the context of strict environmental measures, especially the case of raising oil production by 40 percent. If environmental protection meant that the total domestic production of coal, gas, and oil would not increase significantly in the next decade, then surely conservation measures would be needed beyond the relatively moderate "technical fix" proposals set forth by Mr. Abbotts.[5] (This presumes that generation of nuclear power remains at a low level or is being phased out, which is advocated in the low-energy-growth position.) From this I conclude that all the proposed measures taken together would require radical changes in life style, such as severe restrictions on the use of private automobiles and the rationing of electric power. Another possibility is that America would become even more dependent on imports than it is at present.

Advocates of low energy growth are critical of the corporate system, but no overall consistent vision of our economic future has emerged from this criticism. It is presumably the chief task of Nader's Corporate Accountability Research Group to arrive at an alternative picture of the organization of our economy. The low-growth advocates are more critical of the corporate system than are the mixed-market advocates, yet they stop short of advocating socialism (which would doom them to political irrelevance in America). They are not New Dealers either; they do not envision a powerful executive branch keeping oil companies under control.

If there is a consistency in the low-growth vision of the corporate future, it can be found in a combination of Nader's practice of politics by ad hoc coalitions in combination with his federal chartering proposal, which he describes as follows:

> The bureaucracy created would be as trim and nondiscretionary as possible. [This is not the voice of a New Dealer.] Only the top one thousand interstate corporations—measured by a combination sales, asset size, market percentage,

---

[4] John Abbotts, "Alternative Energy Scenarios" (Washington, D.C.: Public Interest Research Group, 1975), p. 3.

[5] The "technical fix" terminology was introduced by the Energy Policy Project of the Ford Foundation, *A Time to Choose* (Cambridge, Mass.: Ballinger Publishing Company, 1974), Chapter 3.

and number of employees—would be chartered. Manpower would be scaled to confront the basic problem. The kind of charter provisions to be enforced would be as objective as possible: does the firm's market percentage exceed permissible limits? [Nader suggests 12 percent.] Has the corporation provided profit and cost data per division? Did management double its bonus without notifying the shareholders? . . . excessive discretion must be avoided or else the corporate regulatees would successfully shape their supposed regulators—a situation which now obtains.[6]

If a corporation consistently violated its charter, the federal government would have the power to dissolve the offending company. We presume that Nader would not leave the chartering agency in a political vacuum. If it existed, he would create a coalition of public interest groups and sympathetic congressmen to give the chartering agency political backing that would prevent its own dissolution or its becoming a mere bureaucratic rubber stamp.

In the meantime, low-growth advocates tend to push for a wide variety of controls on corporate power without much regard for the formulation of an overall pattern. The same group at different times might call for the chartering of energy companies, divestiture of coal holdings by oil companies, antitrust measures against vertical integration in the oil industry, a publicly owned energy corporation, a consumer protection agency with legal power to intervene in federal energy agency proceedings, participation by citizens in agencies of the executive branch, and so forth.

The low-growth position is one somewhat outside the prevailing tendencies in the political process. I do not want to dwell on inconsistencies within this scenario, however. The low-growth proponents will not get 100 percent of what they want, or even 50 percent. But the debates that they initiate will result in the adoption of some part of their position by society as a whole. It is possible that no more than 120 nuclear power plants will be built in the United States, and if that is the case, Nader's groups and the environmentalist groups will be partly responsible. As noted, these groups are aggressive in bringing the question of the development of solar power to the forefront of discussion, and their activities are at least correlated with the increasing interest in solar energy shown by mainstream decision makers. (ERDA has recently shifted priorities somewhat in the direction of solar development.) The real values of the low-growth positions, then,

---

[6] Ralph Nader and Mark J. Green, eds., *Corporate Power in America* (New York: Grossman Publishers, 1973), p. 83.

are its criticism of existing practices and its initiation of new ideas into the discussion of energy policy.

Public Education about Energy. This position is included because of the activities of the League of Women Voters, an organization that is dedicated primarily to the political education of its members and of the public at large. Gwen Murphree, head of the league's Energy Task Force, makes a cogent point reflecting the league's concern with political education. In her view, public opinion concerning energy questions is at present confused and unstructured. The first thing to do in regard to energy, in her view, is to educate the public to realize that there is an energy crisis and to develop a greater public understanding of what it means.[7]

The need for coherent public opinion concerning energy is a necessary condition for effective national action in this view, which constitutes a separate projection of the future. I think that there is much to this idea. An intelligent chairman of a House committee told me in July 1975 that neither he nor many of his colleagues had a thorough understanding of energy questions. It will not be possible to gain support for billion-dollar construction projects, to raise prices for the purpose of amassing capital or decreasing consumption, to pass conservation measures, or to do whatever is deemed necessary by experts if there is no powerful political backing for such measures. Such backing is in turn dependent upon a coherent public opinion on energy. (I presume that the majority of congressmen do worry about being re-elected, even when no opponent has recently come close to unseating the incumbent.)

There are, of course, smaller public interest groups which have occasionally taken positions on energy matters, but their few stands do not constitute any kind of far-reaching outlook or comprehensive projection for the future.

Organizational Characteristics and Energy Positions

Why do some public interest groups take a mixed-market position while others take a low-energy-growth position? (I am not aware of any public interest group that has taken a development-independence position.[8]) Before discussing what is behind the stands and decisions

---

[7] Gleaned from various remarks made by Murphree at an energy conference sponsored by the American Enterprise Institute, October 2, 1975.

[8] However, the Americans for Energy Independence will probably do this by 1977. It remains to be seen whether that organization will become a public interest group or a new type of economic interest group.

of our seven groups, it is necessary to establish a terminology for describing these groups.

Public interest groups are either membership groups or staff groups. A membership group is one that has a large number of contributors from the general public and a board of directors elected by the members. A staff group, on the other hand, does not have such an elected board, and usually does not have a large number of contributors from the public. (Nader's Public Citizen has 100,000 contributors, however, but no elected board.)

A public interest group can be analyzed in regard to its performance of various functions in the policy process. One is the initiatory function. A group will pick up some idea and begin to push it in the policy process. For example, Lee White of the Consumer Federation of America introduced the idea of a federally owned gas and oil corporation as one which should be considered seriously by Washington policy makers. (Most policy ideas have been around for decades, as this one was. The initiatory function does not involve originating the idea; it refers only to the injection of some proposal into the policy-making process.)

Another function is the aggregative function. Various separate but related policies may be added together or balanced against one another, their separate effects can be analyzed in relation to one another, and eventually they can be combined into a comprehensive statement—"a comprehensive energy platform." Common Cause, the League of Women Voters, and Americans for Energy Independence, for example, seek to do this. In particular, aggregative groups try to balance the important, frequently conflicting values of energy sufficiency, the environment, independence of OPEC, economic prosperity, and political feasibility.

Another function of a public interest group in the policy process is the communications function. After a proposed policy is initiated into the process of political discussion, it needs to be publicized. Decision makers and the politically attentive public must become aware of a proposal and then be persuaded of its value. This requires getting attention to it in the media and coordinating the work of the supporters of the idea. One of Ralph Nader's particular strengths is the ability to draw a great deal of attention from the press to some idea such as the proposal for a moratorium on the construction of nuclear power plants.

As a generalization, public interest groups will perform initiatory functions on matters concerning which group opinion is united. This statement is of greatest interest in discussions of membership groups. Such groups sometimes coalesce around certain values—Common

Cause and the need for reforms in the structure of government, the Sierra Club and the need for conserving the natural environment, Consumers Union and the importance of independent testing of corporate products. Common Cause will initiate in the realm of government reforms but not with respect to energy, except in instances when the two come together (as they do in changing procedures for the granting of leases on government-owned coal lands). The Sierra Club will initiate proposals having to do with the conservation of energy, for example, but will *not* initiate proposals to reform corporate activity in energy production, for these would not be proposals upon which opinion would be unified within their group.

A staff group is likely to have only a small number of decision makers. Sharply conflicting opinions on major group policies are not to be expected because a dissenter would ordinarily force a compromise or leave the staff. But the unity of staff groups does not imply that such groups can initiate a wide range of policies. Such groups tend to be particularly limited in resources and thus do not have the manpower to do research on a wide range of issues. Thus staff groups specialize on a handful of issues which are of particular concern to them, initiating policies only within their areas of specialization. The Energy Task Force of the Consumer Federation of America, consisting of two workers, initiates proposals having to do with oil and gas, but not in other areas. I hypothesize that this relationship between specialization and initiation will hold for the many small public interest groups not discussed in this study.

Another significant tendency can be observed: membership groups, with a high proportion of business persons and/or Republicans as decision makers, will tend toward the mixed-market position, if they seek to put forth a comprehensive energy platform. Common Cause and the League of Women Voters belong in this category. More conservative decision makers will veto the tendency of some liberals to support regulation of gas and oil prices, antitrust action against oil companies, and other anticorporate measures.

Initiatory functions can be performed swiftly and decisively. A press conference can be called immediately; a lawsuit can be initiated with speed. The aggregative function cannot be performed so quickly; policy proposals must first be initiated and their effects at least partially comprehended. Then they must be viewed in relation to one another. (For example, strip mining of Montana coal might at first seem to be a bad idea, but if one were to arrive at a position of phasing out nuclear power, such strip mining might then be advocated as the lesser evil.) With respect to energy, this process seems to take about four years. Neither Common Cause nor the League of Women Voters has set forth a complete energy platform at this time. However, I think Common Cause will do so in 1977 and the League of Women Voters in 1978, which would mean that a period of four years had elapsed in the instance of each between the beginning of organizational concern and the completion of an overall energy statement.

Political scientists often speak of political parties as performing "the function of interest aggregation." By this they mean the formulation of a policy of action which adds together and balances the particular interests within some area of policy. The development-and-independence position of the Ford administration is an example of interest aggregation by the leaders of the Republican party. But what is the alternative energy proposal to be offered by the Democratic party? While Common Cause, perhaps to be joined by other public interest groups, put forth the mixed-market position as an alternative to the policies of the Ford administration, the Democratic party was in confusion. Does the Democratic party favor the deregulation of natural gas? The construction of the plutonium breeder? Who knows? The very questions seem pointless. It seems that public interest groups are now assuming part of the interest-aggregation function that has belonged to American political parties.

Having established a vocabulary for discussing energy positions and the organizational structure of public interest groups, let us now turn to an examination of the decision making of Common Cause on energy questions.

4
COMMON CAUSE

The Approach of a Consensual Membership Organization

Common Cause concentrates on issues having to do with government reform, such as regulation of campaign finance, regulation of lobbying, and requirements for open meetings in government. In 1971 and 1972, Common Cause also engaged in antiwar lobbying, particularly in the House of Representatives, but since that time substantive (as opposed to procedural) goals have been secondary goals of the organization. Thus, Common Cause has not exercised a great deal of influence in energy matters. Its principal activity so far has been active lobbying in the spring of 1975 for the Ways and Means Committee proposal (the so-called Ullman bill) to regulate the use of energy by setting quotas on imported oil and by increasing the federal gasoline tax by twenty cents a gallon in an effort to reduce consumption. Common Cause was also active in lobbying for the Fisher amendment, which would have placed a tax on new cars that are heavy users of gasoline, as opposed to the regulatory approach preferred at present, which is a mandate to automobile manufacturers that the cars produced by a given company must be able to get a stated average number of miles to the gallon.[1] The twenty-cent gas tax failed miserably: 345–72. The Fisher amendment also failed: 235–166.

In spite of these setbacks, Common Cause rapidly developed a comprehensive position on energy during 1975. Energy is seen by the leaders of the organization as likely to take second place only to issues concerning representative government in priority for the future. Since

---

The information and memoranda in this chapter were obtained in the course of field work at the national headquarters of Common Cause during 1975.

[1] See Alan Ehrenhalt, "Energy Lobby: New Voices at Ways and Means," *Congressional Quarterly*, vol. 33 (May 3, 1975), pp. 939–46.

the decision made by Common Cause in April 1975 to support a moratorium on the construction of new nuclear plants, its leaders have seen the necessity of developing positions on issues having to do with coal, which presumably must take up the slack in anticipated production of electric power. This portion of the energy position of Common Cause has not yet been completely worked out, so a comprehensive statement does not yet exist. When such a platform is publicly announced, however, it will have most of the characteristics described earlier under the mixed-market position. It will also contain a statement on production and use of coal (see position 3, above). As noted, such a statement could become the leading alternative to the development-independence position. This would be especially likely if no clear-cut liberal Democratic energy posture were to emerge in the next few years.

How does such an organization as Common Cause, devoted to the enhancement of representation of citizens in government, develop its own policies, such as the mixed-market position on energy? It is important to observe that Common Cause is essentially a consensual organization; more precisely, it is an organization in which the preponderant majorities are of the magnitude of 90 percent. The national staff is not likely to develop lobbying positions that would alienate 20 percent of their national governing board or their members. If ten out of fifty members of the governing board were against a proposed position on energy, that position would either be dropped or modified.

This means that Common Cause could not adopt the low-energy-growth position, even if the staff had concluded that it was a good idea (which the staff in fact did not conclude). Certainly many members of the governing board would refuse to support a statement concerning energy that did not reflect a realistic view of the quantity of energy that will be required in the short run, before solar energy and energy from other new sources can be produced in significant quantities. This position counterbalances the stand of the militant environmentalists (that is, opposition to almost all energy-development projects on environmental grounds). A fraction of the governing board and the members objects strongly to a militant position against nuclear power. Thus, while the governing board did adopt a position in April 1975 favoring a moratorium on the development of nuclear power, if the accumulation of evidence in 1976 and 1977 should suggest strongly that nuclear power is indeed safer and less harmful to the environment than the coal alternative, the board would reverse its position. In other words, the position of Common Cause on nuclear power is less strongly held than those of the Nader organizations and most environmentalist groups, who would not be amenable to

58

reversing their positions with respect to a moratorium on nuclear power.

On the other hand, Common Cause operates in the ideological context of the civic-balance system of beliefs (see Chapter 1). Thus, despite the conclusion of those who do research on the issues for Common Cause that there should be gradual deregulation of the pricing of both oil and natural gas, these positions have not been announced nor have they been supported by lobbying. If such a position were put forth it would anger a significant number of the governing board and of the members of Common Cause, and others in the community of public interest lobbyists as well. According to the idea of civic balance, public interest groups exist to counteract the power of special interests. Oil companies rank close to the top among powerful special interests. According to this system of beliefs, it would be wrong for a public interest group to cooperate even to a limited extent with oil companies in raising the prices of oil and natural gas. Critics of this ideological persuasion do not accept the argument that price increases would conserve supply and lead to a more rational use of scarce resources. Thus, Common Cause will not publicly advocate a position in favor of gradual deregulation of the prices of oil and gas. It would have nothing to gain by doing so.

It is possible that the fraction of the constituency of Common Cause with strong civic-balance beliefs might veto the appearance of a comprehensive statement on energy from Common Cause. In other words, while a majority of the national staff and governing board of Common Cause seems to adhere to the mixed-market position, which includes deregulation of energy prices and consequent price rises (which can be taxed for research funds or for rebates to low-income families), a minority would object to even limited support of the position of the oil companies. Quite a bit of skillful leadership would be needed to overcome such an organizational dilemma.

Common Cause has maintained a considerable degree of unity since consciously emphasizing structure and process issues, that is, issues having to do with representative government, in 1973. In other words, Common Cause has emphasized reforms of the structure and process of government at the national and state levels, such as regulating campaign finances, regulating the activities of lobbyists, requiring disclosure of financial holdings by top officials, requiring that meetings of decision-making bodies be open, reforming the congressional seniority system, and so forth. Persons who care about such issues and feel that reform is needed and who can afford the $15 dues become members of Common Cause (about 275,000). Those who join but find they do not like the positions of Common Cause on government reform issues do not generally renew their memberships. Those who maintain their memberships, however, agree overwhelmingly with the ideas of John Gardner and the staff of Common Cause on issues of government reform.

Gardner and other leaders of Common Cause think that the recent wave of reforms of the structure and process of government enacted at the federal level and in almost all of the states may have reached its crest. At the federal level, for example, if Congress should enact strong legislation regulating the activities of lobbyists, requiring financial disclosures by top-level federal executives, and providing for public financing of congressional elections, this corpus of reform would represent a considerable measure of success of the efforts of Common Cause and its reform-minded allies and could put Common Cause out of business, unless Gardner and his staff should come up with new goals that would appeal to their members.

Common Cause has dealt with this question by developing new types of structure and process issues. During 1976 the organization put forth a major effort to persuade presidential candidates to conduct issues-oriented, rational campaigns. In addition, Gardner and his associates have worked on the idea of developing ways for citizens to direct lobbying activities toward agencies of the federal executive branch.

The commitment of Common Cause to the energy issue represents still another part of the attempt to maintain a strong organization. Of course, Gardner and his staff believe sincerely in the critical nature of energy questions. Gardner was concerned about energy a year ahead of the crowd when he directed his staff to begin the development of a position on energy in the fall of 1972. But if public interest in issues having to do with the accountability of government should wane, Common Cause must be ready to be active on substantive issues (as it was on the Vietnam issue) or else suffer a decline in organizational strength. The leaders of Common Cause see the energy question as providing such a substantive reserve.

Consequently, combining procedure and substance on the energy issue and pursuing ways of reforming the decision-making processes of some of the energy agencies in the federal executive branch are wise courses for Common Cause to follow. The organization has been attempting to do this for more than a year, achieving only limited success. That the project moves slowly is understandable. An economic interest group typically forms friendly ties with the government agency in its field (farmers with the Department of Agriculture, for example), but there has been little experience to show whether a public interest group can interact with an agency and also influence it.

The first attempt of Common Cause was to approach the FEA with its standard measures—such as regulation of the activities of lobbyists and financial disclosure by top executives. Since the FEA is a new agency, it is more amenable to the adoption of new procedures than some others would be. The first FEA administrator, John Sawhill, was interested in Gardner's ideas and agreed to order his top officials to log all their contacts with persons or organizations outside the government. This yielded the interesting datum that top officials of the FEA talked to officials of the energy industry 91 percent of the time and talked to officials of consumer, public interest, and research groups only 6 percent of the time. Such logging of contacts tends to increase the number of contacts that an agency makes with public interest groups, if only so that its officials can be sure that the percentage of such contacts is not embarrassingly low. But such contacts for the purpose of bookkeeping can be pro forma and may not make much difference in the formulation of policies. If such contacts were to be made with public interest lobbyists having strong political backing, however, policies might be changed.

Common Cause regards such logging as useful for defensive purposes:

> The Common Cause proposed regulations would require all Interior Department employees in grades GS-15 or above . . . to keep an open record of all contacts made to them and all written materials given them by outside parties.
>
> These records or "logs" would identify the person making the contact, briefly summarize the matters discussed, and indicate any follow-up action taken. The logs, together with any documents submitted by the outside parties, would be kept in a convenient location within the Department and be available to the public.
>
> Without such procedures, the public and press are unable to gain access to information relating to Interior Department decisions and actions. Private interests, on the other hand, are in daily interaction with Department policymakers through various formal proceedings, ad hoc meetings, office visits, phone calls, et cetera. Data supplied to Interior Department officials by coal and oil companies regulated by the Department, for example, are seldom available or subject to public review.[2]

Common Cause has succeeded in getting the FEA to log outside contacts. It now seeks to generalize this success by petitioning the

[2] "Common Cause Proposed Reforms for the Department of the Interior," Common Cause staff memorandum, July 8, 1975, pp. 3–4.

White House to issue an executive order establishing logging as a standard procedure in all agencies and also establishing new regulations concerning conflicts of interest for all agencies.

In the spring of 1975, Common Cause developed a technique that combines its twin interests in accountability of the executive branch and energy policy making. The new technique is to persuade a presidential appointee to commit himself publicly to certain reforms during the Senate's confirmation process. Common Cause has used a similar technique to secure public commitments from congressional candidates during the 1972, 1974, and 1976 elections. Representatives of Common Cause interviewed congressional candidates, questioning them about their positions on such issues as regulation of campaign spending, requiring that legislative meetings be open, and other issues from the agenda of Common Cause. Securing public commitments is an effective technique if some publicity apparatus is available for the purpose of exposing departures from the commitment. Common Cause puts great emphasis on its relationship with the press, and thus in many cases it can embarrass an official who does not follow through on publicly stated promises.

While Common Cause used this technique to some extent during the confirmation hearings for FEA administrators Sawhill and Zarb, much more emphasis was placed on obtaining commitments from Interior Secretary-designate Stanley Hathaway during his confirmation hearings in May 1975. Common Cause did not take a position on whether Hathaway should be confirmed; instead it submitted a list of questions to the nominee regarding his future policies with respect to conflict of interest, logging of outside contacts, leasing policies, and openness to the public. Senator Henry Jackson, chairman of the Senate Committee on Interior and Insular Affairs, liked the Common Cause list and directed the nominee to answer the questions; Mr. Hathaway did so, although sometimes in general terms. The list of questions and Hathaway's answers to them were placed in the Interior Committee's confirmation report, thus constituting an informal commitment on Hathaway's part. Unfortunately, Hathaway served as secretary of the interior for only six weeks because the lengthy and controversial process of his confirmation had induced in him a state of mental depression which forced him to resign. (Hathaway was opposed by environmentalist groups.) Limits to the Common Cause technique of securing public commitment were demonstrated during the process of confirmation of Thomas Kleppe (October 1975), who did not respond at length to the questions of Common Cause before he was confirmed as secretary of the interior in what was a particularly quick proceeding for confirmation of a cabinet officer.

The technique of obtaining commitments during the confirmation process is an important one, and it will be used frequently by Common Cause in future proceedings, at least when the committee conducting the hearings likes the list of questions. I will include below, in Appendix A, the record of Common Cause's questions and Hathaway's responses to give some of the flavor of this new technique.

Other Energy Positions of Common Cause

Common Cause was a prominent part of the lobbying coalition which succeeded in getting the oil-depletion allowance repealed in the spring of 1975. One of the major congressional addresses on this topic was drafted by members of the staff of Common Cause, for example. The fact that Common Cause was able to overcome internal opposition and take a stand with respect to the oil-depletion allowance is another illustration of the recent unpopularity of oil companies. The governing board of Common Cause is badly split on tax-reform issues: Representatives of business defend the present capital-gains deductions, representatives of privately financed universities defend the present system of deductions for charitable gifts, and so forth. The oil-depletion allowance, however, had no defenders on the governing board and Common Cause was able to lobby against it.

Conservation is basic to the energy position of Common Cause, but unlike the advocates of the low-growth position, Common Cause is also concerned about the need for increasing the supply of energy during the next ten years. The basic Common Cause memo (reprinted in its entirety in Appendix B) begins as follows:

> Energy conservation is the key to the success of any energy program. But successful conservation will not eliminate the need to develop additional energy sources. The Energy Policy Project of the Ford Foundation pointed out that even in its limited growth scenario (1.9 percent growth per year), energy supply will need to be approximately 28 percent larger in 1985 than in 1975.

As noted, Common Cause recognizes the need to develop our domestic coal resources (see Appendix B).

The Common Cause position on conservation of energy was summarized by John Gardner in a statement to the House Ways and Means Committee, submitted on March 11, 1975, as part of his testimony in support of the ill-fated Ullman bill:

> So one ingredient in the energy crisis is the vulnerability stemming from our excessive dependence on imports. *There*

is only one short-term solution to that vulnerability: a sharp reduction in our wasteful consumption of energy. . . . An oil import quota system combined with fair allocation and a progressive gasoline tax is the central element of a "conserve now" energy policy. Other steps must be taken that will ensure energy conservation over the longer term. Legislated standards for gasoline efficient automobiles, increased funding for mass transit, measures to reduce waste in the heating and air conditioning of buildings, energy-efficient labeling, elimination of promotional discounts for big energy users, and increased R & D funding for energy-saving technology and methods are examples of actions that would result in significant energy savings. Commercial and industrial conservation goals by sector should be developed and monitored by an appropriate federal agency, and suitable incentives or penalties enacted if they prove necessary.

Tax policies should be reviewed or amended to ensure that they encourage energy conservation. For example, the deductibility of state/local gasoline taxes for federal income tax purposes should be eliminated. A tax on heavy, high-horsepower automobiles should be enacted. Tax incentives can be developed to encourage energy-saving residential heating and cooling methods. And, very important, tax adjustments should be made to ensure that low-income citizens are not confronted with budget-breaking energy prices.[3]

In discussions with the national governing board on energy, Gardner always mentions that increases in domestic production of energy should not be made at the expense of environmental standards. The environmental issue is dear to the hearts of Common Cause members. The environment is always close to the top in polls of the membership concerning priorities that they would give to various issues (though government reform is clearly the number one preference of the membership). I expect that Common Cause will have trouble in squaring its support for environmental safeguards with its movement toward support of increasing coal production to take up the slack in production of energy. In particular, the issue of strip mining of Western coal is one on which it is difficult to balance environmental safeguards (at least as they are defined by environmentalists) and increased production of energy.

One interesting position of Common Cause is the result of the interaction of the organization's consensual decision making, its em-

---

[3] "Statement of John W. Gardner, chairman of Common Cause, on Energy Policy before the Ways and Means Committee of the House of Representatives, March 11, 1975," pp. 4, 5–6, emphasis in the original. Available from Common Cause, 2030 M St., N.W., Washington, D.C. 20036.

phasis on structure and process reforms, and the nuclear moratorium issue. There should be no doubt in the reader's mind that government reform is still the number one priority of Common Cause. For 1976 Common Cause marshalled its organizational resources for a major "Campaign '76" program, generally to induce presidential candidates to conduct issue-oriented campaigns. At the same time, statewide referenda on proposals for a nuclear moratorium in California and six other states were placed on the ballot by initiative petitions. The national staff and governing board of Common Cause did not want these state Common Cause organizations to campaign for the nuclear moratorium initiatives, however, and did not want them to use the name of Common Cause even for endorsement purposes.

One reason for this is that a hotly contested referendum on the nuclear moratorium issue would use up the time and the motivational resources of state Common Cause organizations. There would be little left over for the issue having first priority, the "Campaign '76" program. A second reason is that endorsement of a nuclear moratorium would be internally divisive. In a poll of Common Cause members taken in March 1976, it was found that 60 percent of the members would support a Common Cause position which "resisted all efforts to expand the use of nuclear power plants," but 30 percent would oppose such a position, with 10 percent undecided. Common Cause has never knowingly lobbied for something opposed by 30 percent of its members. Any further support from Common Cause for a moratorium on the production of nuclear energy is sure to be cautious, probably emphasizing the structure and process approach of reforming governmental procedures relevant to nuclear power legislation. For example, Common Cause called for abolishing the congressional Joint Committee on Atomic Energy, a friend of nuclear power. But certainly support of Common Cause for a nuclear moratorium is not the militant support that is given by a Ralph Nader or by the Friends of the Earth organization.

In conclusion, I have described Common Cause as performing an aggregative function in the energy field. Common Cause is a group whose number one priority is issues having to do with government accountability. With respect to energy, Common Cause has not been an active force in initiating new issues, except in the area of its specialization—government procedures—where its insistence on regulation of conflicts of interest and logging of extragovernmental contacts and its developing concern for regulation of oil and coal leases constitute a new public interest group technique. Another aspect of its lobbying in the executive branch is securing public commitments about energy policy from nominees during confirmation hearings.

The staff of Common Cause does not like to develop a lobbying position unless it has a near consensus of support from its national governing board and the support of the great majority of its members who may be concerned about the issue. Such consensual operation has not prevented Common Cause from being active and effective on issues of government reform, because almost all the members of Common Cause agree strongly with the national staff on such issues. But in the case of the energy issue, potential opposing groups exist among the governing board and the members. Common Cause cannot take a militant low-energy-growth position, because part of its board would object. (Its staff is not attracted to such a position in any event.) On the other hand, the staff of Common Cause cannot do anything in support of gradual deregulation of the prices of oil and natural gas, because part of its board, membership, and public interest group constituency would object to any lobbying on the side of the oil companies on what is seen as a question of special interests versus public interests. Thus, the selection by Common Cause of public interests that it will advocate is shaped by organizational imperatives.

But this is not to belittle Common Cause. What else could be expected in the world of politics? And, in point of fact, Common Cause is successfully aggregating a pattern of energy positions corresponding to the mixed-market position. In doing so it set forth workable alternatives to the development-independence policies of the Ford administration.

The first three appendixes to this book are important to the understanding of the positions of Common Cause on energy. Appendix A is the list of questions put to nominee Hathaway by Common Cause and his answers. Appendix B is the basic Common Cause staff memorandum on energy, which presupposes a strong conservationist position, such as that described in the foregoing quotation from Gardner. This memorandum indicates the concern of Common Cause for balancing various interests and priorities having to do with energy. Since it was written in April 1975, however, it should not be taken as the final statement of Common Cause on the question of energy. It will probably be revised every few years. Appendix C contains parts of a memorandum written in response to the great volume of criticism received by Common Cause for supporting the moratorium on the licensing of construction of nuclear power plants. The memorandum gives some feeling of the willingness of the staff to consider more than one point of view.

5
SIX PUBLIC INTEREST GROUPS AND ENERGY

Nader Organizations

Ralph Nader, one of the most remarkable figures of our time, has institutionalized himself in about fifteen separate public interest groups in Washington. In addition, local Nader organizations exist on the campuses of perhaps thirty universities. The Nader system of beliefs epitomizes civic-balance theory. Nader and his followers are ever on the watch for victimization of the interests of the public at large by corporate and bureaucratic "selfish interests." Most of Nader's public career has been in the fields of consumer affairs, environmental concerns, and government reform—fields that are particularly susceptible to the problems of representing interests of large publics that are difficult to organize. In such fields of policy, the claim that widespread public interests need an advocate is plausible. One can say that widespread interests having to do with personal health and safety, consumer financial affairs, and the concerns of citizens not yet born are frequently unrepresented. Nader has made himself the advocate of such interests. Since energy is another matter concerning which the argument that widespread interests are unrepresented is plausible, it is not surprising that Nader is becoming very active with respect to the energy question also.

Critics refer to Nader as a "self-appointed" spokesman for the consumer, but such a description can be misleading. Nader should be regarded as a free-lance politician. He has a constituency which gives him support, just as other politicians do. This is how Nader

---

The research in this chapter is based on one or two interviews with energy workers within each organization, subsequent telephone calls during the writing process, inspection of energy-related documents produced by each organization, and general knowledge of public interest groups gained from my previous interests in this area of politics.

raises $2 million a year for his activities. About 100,000 persons contribute to Public Citizen, Inc., the Nader fund-raising agency. (Such contributions amount to $1.1 million a year, but about 35 percent of that sum goes for mailing expenses.) A figure of charismatic appeal, Nader is a sure sell-out as a public speaker and can therefore command $3,500 for an appearance wherever he appears. (It is my guess that he grosses about $400,000 a year by giving about 100 such speeches.) His profits from book sales, newspaper columns, foundation grants, and gifts amount to about half a million dollars. With this income Nader can finance an enterprise encompassing research, lobbying, writing, media relations, and political coordination that can multiply his own personal efforts to protect public interests.[1]

A distinctive talent of Nader's is his flair for publicizing issues. He is particularly adept at managing the communications function of public interest groups. He maintains good relationships with reporters, whom he can assist by giving them the product of the latest investigations of his research staff. Nader can help congressmen, particularly those with liberal constituencies, who may want to sponsor recent Nader ideas in the House or the Senate. Working with Nader can give a congressman a lot of favorable publicity, which can help his career by building his image as a champion of the rights of the consumer. Senator Warren Magnuson, Democrat of Washington, for example, was re-elected by a disappointingly small margin in 1962, which led him to take on the role of consumer advocate in the Senate, in cooperation with Nader, a factor in his winning substantial victories in 1968 and 1974. Similarly Representative Benjamin Rosenthal, Democrat of New York, probably ranks among the top ten members of the House in volume of favorable publicity in the national media, publicity that he receives as a result of being a chief supporter of such Nader measures as the Consumer Protection Agency bill. Rosenthal's dynamic image undoubtedly had something to do with his re-election in 1974 by a majority of 79 percent in a district in which Nixon received 50 percent of the vote in 1972.

Nader and a congressman who is chairman of a congressional subcommittee can collaborate in getting national publicity for some matter by holding a hearing of the subcommittee. Nader's testimony at the hearing is sure to attract attention from the press, thereby making the congressman look good and giving the stamp of government authority to Nader's concerns.

Nader has that elusive quality which can be termed "media stardom." He projects himself well through the media, particularly

[1] See Theodore Jacqueney, "Nader Network Switches Focus to Legal Action, Congressional Lobbying," *National Journal*, vol. 5 (June 9, 1973), pp. 840–49.

television, having a strong appeal to typical Americans and, more important, radiating a quality of excitement. Because the masses are interested in the lives of media stars, almost everything they do is publicized. If a media star calls a press conference, it automatically receives attention. As such a celebrity, Nader does not have to engage in any elaborate planning or strategy to publicize an issue. Publicity comes naturally to the issues about which he is concerned because these issues are ipso facto newsworthy.

The characteristics of media stardom can be seen in the current politics of the construction of nuclear power plants. Opposition to nuclear plants did not begin with Nader; it began with various local coalitions opposing the construction of nuclear plants in their neighborhoods and with criticisms of nuclear power by such scientists as John W. Gofman and Arthur R. Tamplin.[2] The antinuclear issue was pushed by the more aggressive environmentalist groups, such as Friends of the Earth. Nader, along with the Sierra Club, was part of the second wave of the antinuclear movement. Environmentalists and scientists were active on the issue by 1970. Nader's activity began on March 1, 1973, when he testified against nuclear power before Congress; he joined the Friends of the Earth in a suit, filed on May 31, 1973, to close down twenty of the thirty-two nuclear power plants then in operation because of alleged deficiencies in the emergency core cooler system (to prevent "meltdowns").[3] By late 1974, however, preventing the construction of nuclear plants was at the top of the list of Nader's political priorities, second only to the establishment of a consumer protection agency. Nader's interest in the matter is automatically rewarded with attention in the media, so now a Nader lobbyist working in coalitions with those whose antinuclear stands predated Nader's has to counteract the resentment of those who were the first to broach the issue but do not now get widespread public credit for it. Meanwhile, reporters happily write "Nader versus Nuclear" stories. Because of Nader's media stardom, the press and television have given Nader the new role of the nation's number one critic of nuclear power.

In this example one can see that there was a first wave of activity by local groups, scientists, and aggressive environmental groups which performed the *initiatory* function. Then there was a second wave of criticism, including that of Nader and the Sierra Club. In the second

---

[2] Richard S. Lewis, *The Nuclear-Power Rebellion: Citizens vs. the Atomic Industrial Establishment* (New York: The Viking Press, 1972); Steven Ebbin and Raphael Kasper, *Citizen Groups and the Nuclear Power Controversy* (Cambridge, Mass.: MIT Press, 1974).

[3] Claude E. Barfield, "Broad Campaign against Nuclear Power Begins with Nader Suit on Reactor Safety," *National Journal*, vol. 5 (June 9, 1973), pp. 850–51.

wave it was principally Nader who performed the *communications* function. Finally, Common Cause, and perhaps the League of Women Voters, will incorporate a position on nuclear energy into an overall energy platform, thereby performing an *aggregative* function.

Nader and His Staff Make the Decisions. Ralph Nader dislikes bigness in institutions generally and therefore established separate small organizations, now numbering about fifteen, rather than unite all his activities in the work of a single lobbying and research conglomerate. What would be a department of Common Cause is a separate organization within the Nader network. There are five Nader organizations that are sufficiently concerned with the question of energy to deserve mention. They are Public Citizen, Inc., the fund-raising-by-mail outfit; Congress Watch, the office from which most of Nader's lobbyists work; Critical Mass, the Washington office that coordinates local antinuclear efforts; the Tax Reform Research Group, which handles lobbying before the Ways and Means Committee, including lobbying on energy legislation incorporated within tax bills; and the Public Interest Research Group of Washington, D.C., which is not to be confused with state and university organizations having the same name (New York PIRG, Penn State PIRG, et cetera).

The first four groups are supported by funds raised through mass mailings and are not eligible for tax-deductible contributions because of their lobbying activities. I presume that the national Public Interest Research Group and other similar Nader research groups avoid lobbying and are thereby eligible for tax-deductible contributions. Such organizational diversification must be rewarded with an occasional tax-deductible grant. In contrast, someone who gave a substantial gift to the Common Cause issues-research staff for research on energy could not then deduct the gift from his taxable income.

Each separate Nader organization employs only a few persons, however. At any given time no more than ten to fifteen persons are likely to be working with Nader on energy policy. In the last analysis, Nader is the boss of this staff of lobbyists and researchers. He hires them, he provides them with funds, and he could fire them if they disagreed with him severely. Decision making on energy within the Nader organizations is therefore simple: Nader makes the decisions in consultation with his staff.

But this does not imply that Nader has absolute freedom of action with respect to energy. He is constrained by limitation of resources, for one thing. Nader is expected by his constituency to be "the consumer crusader," a role he plays gladly. But this means that he is expected to stay on top of other consumer issues besides energy. In the last analysis, Nader must be a consumer generalist or severely disappoint much of his constituency. Since Nader can devote only so much time to energy issues, he must specialize. Accordingly, he focuses his efforts on the issue of nuclear power, which is indeed central to policy making with respect to energy and which is also the issue upon which Nader's journalistic talents of investigation, criticism, and moral censure have the strongest effect. But Nader and his associates do not have the resources to master issues having to do with coal and must therefore follow the lead of other organizations, such as the Environmental Policy Center and the Sierra Club, on this emerging group of energy issues. In this sense, Nader is limited.

Critics of Nader point out that he has only limited expertise with respect to nuclear power. One can clearly say that Nader has "mastered" the nuclear issue, however, in that he knows which arguments are most damaging to the pronuclear side. On the other hand, Nader lacks such a mastery of coal issues, but this he could surely gain after some study.

Nader's people, along with the Friends of the Earth, now take the lead among public interest lobbies in Washington on nuclear issues. (Lobbying at the state level may be more important in shaping events having to do with these issues than lobbying in Washington. In particular, if referenda prohibiting the construction of nuclear plants except under closely restricted circumstances were to be passed in California and a few other states, and if such referenda were found to be legal under federal-state preemption doctrines, then state organizations could claim primary responsibility for stopping nuclear construction.)

As noted earlier, Nader was not an initiator on the antinuclear issue, but he now plays a central publicizing and coordinating role in relation to it. He convened Critical Mass conventions of antinuclear activists in Washington in November 1974 and November 1975. A meeting of a steering committee in February 1975 set up the Critical Mass office in Washington to coordinate local antinuclear activities between conventions. About 300 persons attended the first Critical Mass convention; about 1,000 attended the second. This is indicative of the growing strength of the antinuclear movement.

What can a Washington office do to coordinate dozens of autonomous local movements? I cannot say exactly what Nader is doing in this respect, but I can mention some of the things that would need to be done. Experience in California indicates that voters may pass a referendum, only to have it thrown out by the courts as unconstitutional. Antinuclear referenda are not exceptional; I heard four different accounts of the legality of the failed 1976 California referendum to impose a moratorium on the construction of nuclear plants. Legal advice would be important to a national coordination effort. Another function could be the distribution of technical arguments from antinuclear scientists. Still another would be the circulation of rebuttals to common pronuclear arguments. Knowledge of the people most likely to support the antinuclear position could be traded. Nader personnel were surprised to discover that both small marketers of fuel oil and members of the John Birch Society tend to be adamantly antinuclear. Such nonobvious information is quite useful to a local organizer. Much of the coordinating function is performed in the Nader organizations by the publication of a twelve-page monthly newspaper, *Critical Mass*, an interesting journal which gives the reader a sense that he is part of a burgeoning nationwide movement by chronicling antinuclear activities in various areas; the latest antinuclear arguments; the latest information on Washington lobbying, with congressional voting charts; articles on the possibilities for conservation of energy; information on alternative sources of energy, especially solar power; inside information on what ERDA, FEA, and other federal agencies are up to; criticism of leading pronuclear advocates; and an annotated reading list of recent energy research, emphasizing federal documents and reports by public interest research groups.[4]

National coordination means that local groups can benefit from Nader's experience as a political strategist. It was discovered, for example, that as part of the procedures for obtaining an operating permit for a nuclear plant, electric power companies had to file plans with the Atomic Energy Commission to show how the local community would be evacuated in case of melt-down or other release of a substantial amount of radioactivity into the plant's environment. Nader is now suing the successor agency to the AEC, the Nuclear Regulatory Commission, for public release of these documents. If they are released, it will be a propaganda disaster for the pronuclear forces. Nader will send the evaluation documents to local antinuclear groups, who will then call this sensational story to the attention of local newspapers and television stations.[5]

In other words, Nader's central function in relation to the energy question is communication on the subject of the antinuclear moratorium. However, Nader and his staff have been initiators in other areas of policy, particularly in the field of consumer safety, as witness

[4] *Critical Mass* is obtainable by subscription (price varies with category) by writing to Critical Mass, P.O. Box 1538, Washington, D.C., 20013.
[5] Lou Sirico, "Citizens Demand Improved Evacuation Procedures," *Critical Mass*, vol. 1 (August 1975), p. 5.

their well-known criticism of automobiles, meat-packing plants, and so forth. I expect that Nader organizations will be initiators on the subject of solar power. *Critical Mass* is full of favorable references to solar power. This seems to be the type of issue that Nader likes—one of sponsoring an idea which could prove valuable to the public at large but which does not yet have strong backing from economic interests. In addition, Nader lobbyists recognize the fact that they need to push the development of some kind of energy in order to make their antidevelopment positions more credible to Congress and to the politically aware public. (There is an irony in this. Fifty years from now, if all goes well with America and if our institutions don't change radically, there will be a well-financed group of lobbyists for solar power, lobbying for their vested interest against the latest challenger, which is likely to be fusion power. In other words, Nader and other contemporary public interest groups may now be lobbying for tomorrow's selfish interests, in some cases.)

Nader might take an initiatory role and become the leader of the lobbying coalition on another question related to energy. This is a group of issues just becoming prominent that I think will attain primary importance, particularly if a liberal Democrat is elected President and the liberals control both houses of Congress. Among the ideas in this group are a federal mandate to divide the large oil companies into functional units, each concerned with one function of the industry—production, transportation, refining, marketing and so forth; a mandate to divest the oil companies of coal and uranium holdings; and the formation of a federally owned oil and gas corporation —that is, a yardstick enterprise to compete with privately owned business. Nader personnel already have lobbied for the first and the third of these measures, but since they have not yet received serious consideration from Congress, this lobbying effort was not of major scope. (The Abourezk Amendment, sponsored by the Democrat from South Dakota, succeeded in getting the votes of forty-five senators in October 1975 in support of breaking up the large oil companies.[6] This measure appeared on the political scene suddenly, taking almost everyone, including the Nader lobbyists, by surprise. It was not discussed at length, and thus in spite of its having received the votes of forty-five senators, vertical antitrust measures against oil companies are still a long way from congressional ratification.)

There are three reasons that Nader might assume leadership with respect to government policy toward the corporate structure of the oil industry. First, Nader is already a leading critic of the structure of

---

[6] *Congressional Record*, October 8, 1975, pp. S17832–64.

American industry, in that such criticism is one of his top priorities and Nader's criticisms receive wide publicty. It would be natural for Nader to apply his general criticisms of the structure of American corporations to the oil industry in particular. Second, at this time the oil industry is extraordinarily unpopular with the general public.[7] No one is more conscious of this than the oil companies themselves, as can be seen from recent newspaper and television advertising of the industry. Advocacy of antitrust action in the oil sector would enhance Nader's popularity with his particular constituency and with the general public, and he would lose few supporters, since defenders of the oil industry are already critical of him. Third, advocacy of this issue would protect Nader's reputation with other public interest groups as an initiator of public interest causes. While the environmentalist groups and individuals who pioneered in the criticism of the nuclear industry surely understand Nader's publicizing role, there is nevertheless bound to be some resentment against Nader for getting all the publicity in an area in which others have worked for years. Thus there is pressure on Nader to take the lead in introducing new measures concerned with energy. Advocacy of reorganizing the oil industry would fulfill this expectation.

Nader Organizations: Conclusion. In addition to assuming a leading role on questions of nuclear energy, lobbyists of the Nader organizations are active on a number of other leading energy questions before the Congress. They oppose the deregulation of old oil and natural gas. They supported the Fisher Amendment, which would have taxed new cars having high gas consumption, and they opposed the twenty-cent federal gas tax in the Ullman proposals of May 1975. Nader supports the Udall measures proposed by Congressman Udall to control stripmining, although the leadership in this area of lobbying has been assumed by several other groups. Nader strongly supports measures that are intended to develop alternative sources of energy, such as solar and geothermal power, fusion processes, and even wind power.

Energy conservation measures are also strongly supported by Nader, although in 1976 such proposals got lost in the shuffle of election-year politics. I expect that Nader will be negative about the possibilities of shale oil development and coal-to-gas conversion plants in the light of the dangers posed by these technologies to the environment in semiarid Western regions.

In summary, the totality of Nader policies amounts to a low-

---

[7] Robert Walters, "Petroleum and the People," *National Journal*, vol. 7 (October 18, 1975), p. 1457.

energy-growth position. A moratorium on nuclear development, government regulation of oil and gas prices at present levels, scrupulous environmental restrictions on oil and coal development, little development of Western coal or oil shale, and division of the big oil companies would make it difficult to increase domestic production of energy. Nader's staff recognizes the restrictions on energy development that follow from the sum of their policies. They propose aggressive development of solar power and major initiatives in the field of conservation, but it is difficult to see how such measures could make up the difference in energy development in the short run of ten to fifteen years. Nader is fond of pointing out that Sweden and West Germany now have a standard of living equivalent to the American standard, while these countries use only about half as much energy per capita as we do. It is also true, however, that Swedes and Germans drive fewer miles (25 percent of American consumption of energy is in transportation) largely because their cities are more compactly laid out. Homes and industrial plants in Europe are designed with a concern for conservation of energy, because historically prices have been higher in Europe. Our inheritance of building construction and urban sprawl sets significant limits on conservation of energy. (Of course there is much that we can do by means of simple measures, such as speed limits of fifty-five miles per hour, campaigns to turn out the lights and to lower the thermostat, and the adoption of energy-conserving building codes. The political will to go beyond such simple measures is now lacking, however, and problems are thereby posed for the low-energy-growth position.)

While the low-energy-growth position has problems, the main significance of Nader's efforts in respect to energy lies in the nuclear moratorium proposal. At present the whole nuclear power effort is in trouble, primarily for economic reasons, secondarily for political reasons. Nader's skill at publicizing issues and his technical assistance to local antinuclear groups have significantly increased the political barriers to the construction of nuclear power plants. And perhaps it is correct to expect that Nader will have significant influence in accelerating the development of solar power and in regulating the corporate structure of the oil industry. There are indications, however, that Nader's lobbying effectiveness, particularly in the House of Representatives, leaves much to be desired. The statement of Frank Ikard, president of the American Petroleum Institute, that "Common Cause and Nader are the two most powerful groups in the United States"[8] is hyperbole. Thus Nader's number one priority, the proposal

[8] Alan Ehrenhalt, "Energy Lobby: New Voices at Ways and Means," *Congressional Quarterly*, vol. 33 (May 3, 1975), p. 940.

LIBRARY
OF
MOUNT ST. MARY'S
COLLEGE
MARYLAND

for a consumer protection agency, squeaked through the House on November 6, 1975, by a vote of 208–199, even though it had passed by margins better than 2-1 in 1971 and 1974.[9] This result shows that Nader's lobbying capacity in one branch of Congress is distinctly limited. Another bit of evidence to this effect is derived from an interview conducted with a leading liberal strategist in the House on July 31, 1975. This congressman noted spontaneously that the Nader lobbyists were botching the job on the consumer protection agency. He thought that the Nader group did not understand the legislative process in the House, contrasting unfavorably with Common Cause in this respect. He observed that the consumer protection agency should by then have passed the House and that the bill seemed to be in real trouble. On the other hand, this congressman, who will have no trouble being re-elected, specifically asked not to be quoted by name in thus criticizing the Nader lobbying effort. He respected Nader's skills in publicity (he feared embarrassment), but he did not think so highly of the capabilities of the Nader lobbyists in political strategy. A well-known chairman of a congressional committee noted in an interview (July 1975) that before the 1972 election, many of his colleagues were fearful of the booklets on the individual congressmen put out by Nader's Congress Project, but it seemed that the booklets made little difference in the great majority of congressional races. The chairman commented that since Nader could not ordinarily affect a congressional election, his reputation for political clout was thereby reduced. (Nader campaigning in person, however, would be many times more effective than a booklet issued by one of his researchers. Nader threatened to campaign against three senators who helped block the consumer protection agency proposal in a cloture vote in 1974, but so far as I know, he did not carry out this threat.)

I conclude that Nader has a great deal of influence on events through his skills at publicity and that this influence will be significant in the struggle over nuclear power. These communications skills could prove influential in connection with the development of solar power and antitrust action against the oil companies, but the influence of Nader lobbyists on other energy questions is more limited.

To use the vocabulary of Chapter 3, Nader organizations are staff organizations in which Nader makes the basic decisions. Nader is expected by his constituency to be a consumer generalist, and many of his personal and organizational resources of money and time must be spent with that in mind. Nader's activity with respect to energy, then, is subject to specialization, and the focus of that specialization is the

---

[9] Prudence Crewdson, "House Gives Consumer Agency Slim Margin," *Congressional Quarterly*, vol. 33 (November 15, 1975), pp. 2451–56.

issue of nuclear power. This issue is at the heart of energy decisions and is congruent with Nader's previous concerns of protecting public health and safety. While Nader has frequently performed the initiatory function on other questions of public policy, his activity so far on energy questions has been concentrated on the communications function, especially on the issue of nuclear power. There are pressures on him to initiate proposals having to do with energy, however, and I think that he will do so. The energy stands of Nader organizations add up to a low-energy-growth position, although Nader people do stress the importance of conservation and of developing solar power.

The League of Women Voters

The League of Women Voters was founded in 1920 as an institutionalization of the woman suffrage movement; its main purpose at that time was to promote political education among women so that they could effectively exercise their franchise. From the start, the league has been an active lobbying organization in Washington. In the early 1930s the size of its membership and its organizational strength declined sharply. This decline was turned around in the late 1930s, however, when the league began its current emphasis on good-government issues combined with determined efforts to inform the public about political issues and elections. The league forged a new strength and unity around this structure and process emphasis in a fashion comparable to the unity that Common Cause built around these issues in the 1970s. In the last two decades, the league has become known primarily for its efforts at public education, including its efforts to make its members better informed. It is now known secondarily as a proponent of "women's issues" and for its stands on other issues, such as its early support for reciprocal trade legislation and for normalizing the relationship between the United States and mainland China.

The league is similar to other membership public interest groups in drawing upon a constituency of white upper middle-class persons. According to an internal survey of the league, 68 percent of its members hold college degrees, while 50 percent of the husbands of members are professionals and another 27 percent are in business.[10] The league now has approximately 140,000 members, and about 3,000 of them men. About four members in ten are more than fifty years of age; one member in fourteen is under thirty. Active members, how-

---

[10] Albert H. Cantril and Susan Davis Cantril, *The Report of the Findings of the League Self-Study*, publication no. 545 of the League of Women Voters of the United States (Washington, D.C.: League of Women Voters, 1974).

ever, are younger on the whole than the average member. In the fall of 1973, about half the members were found to be Democrats, a third were independents, and a sixth were Republicans.[11] The league has about 1,300 local chapters; the local chapter is the basic organizational unit, although there are state chapters, metropolitan-area chapters, inter-league organizations (ad hoc confederations of local units), and the national organization. The national league is split in two: the League of Women Voters of the United States and the League of Women Voters Education Fund. The latter unit was separated so that tax-deductible gifts could be made to the Education Fund for research purposes, since the league itself maintains a lobbying staff. The income of the national league for 1974–75 was $1.1 million; the income of the Education Fund at that time was $964,000.[12]

The league is a very democratic organization, in both senses in which the term *democratic* is used in the current literature of political science. In one sense, a democratic organization is one in which the leaders are controlled by the followers.[13] It would be highly unlikely that the national staff or board of directors of the league would get out of step with the majority of the members, because the national staff is financed by assessments from the local chapters, and there is a continuing, well organized process of communication between the national staff and the local chapters. In another sense, a *democratic* organization is one in which individual members or citizens participate in public decisions that involve comprehension of the issues and rational discussion leading up to the choices made by the group or the public.[14] A primary goal of the league has always been enhancement of the political education of its members, and therefore, by its own ideology, the league has developed a formal process whereby members set the lobbying agenda of the national league, discuss the issues involved, and make collective decisions, ordinarily at the local chapter level. The league is a federal organization, which means that state and local chapters can lobby on issues on which the national organization has not taken a position. (Of course, lobbying activity by local units cannot contradict a national consensus, the apt term for the league's national decision-making process.) Thus, while the national organization is not even close to taking a position on the issue of a nuclear moratorium, the Oregon and Wisconsin leagues have taken stands in

---

[11] *The National Voter*, vol. 24 (March-April 1974), pp. 1–2. This is the journal of the League of Women Voters of the United States.

[12] *Annual Report: LWVUS & LWVEF*, 1974–75 edition.

[13] See Robert A. Dahl, *Who Governs?* (New Haven: Yale University Press, 1961).

[14] See Robert J. Pranger, *The Eclipse of Citizenship: Power and Participation in Contemporary Politics* (New York: Holt, Rinehart and Winston, 1968).

favor of the moratorium, and the Oregon group is actively pursuing this position.

The league appears to be a significant force in affecting public opinion among the 5 to 10 percent of the public that is the most attentive to political issues, particularly among upper middle-class opinion leaders. Thus, in the only published political science analysis of the league that I have seen, the authors found that the league evidently affected public opinion on the reciprocal trade issue in the early 1950s, but they concluded that they could not estimate the lobbying effectiveness of the league in regard to Congress. According to them, the league put forth

> a prodigious output of activity. . . . During 1954, the League must have been by several orders of magnitude the most active group to be found on either side of the trade controversy. The intensity of involvement of the League members matched the extent of its activities. . . . The League's local studies [of the impact of reciprocal trade legislation] . . . constituted a major source of new information in the controversy of 1953–1955. . . . How effective was all this activity? By its very nature, the League's activity is difficult to evaluate. Its efforts were broad and involved general public enlightenment, which might or might not have some influence at a later day in a roundabout fashion.[15]

Another study indicates that officials of women's groups name the league third most frequently when asked which organizations they work with to influence public policy, indicating that other lobbying groups of women have found the league to be reasonably effective.[16] In addition, the structure of the league and the characteristics of its members are conducive to gaining political influence with Congress. The league is an organization of politically active persons that is represented in all states and in the great majority of congressional districts. Such geographical dispersion increases an organization's influence with Congress. Moreover, most congressmen surely recognize that league chapters contain opinion leaders active in the politics of local communities, who are thus in a position to enhance or to harm a congressman's reputation. It thus would seem that most congressmen would give lobbyists of the league a respectful hearing. The effec-

---

[15] Raymond A. Bauer, Ithiel de Sola Pool, and Lewis Anthony Dexter, *American Business and Public Policy* (New York: Atherton Press, 1963), pp. 388, 389, 391, 392–93. This volume received the Woodrow Wilson Award of the American Political Science Association as the best political science book of its year.

[16] Anne N. Costain, "A Social Movement Lobbies: Women's Liberation and Pressure Politics." Paper given at the annual meeting of the Southern Political Science Association, November 1975, p. 17.

tiveness of the league, however, is weakened by its lobbying for several types of issues at the same time. All in all, the Washington lobby of the league seems to have moderate influence over congressmen, but less influence than the AFL-CIO or Common Cause have, for example.

After the energy crisis brought on by the Arab oil embargo, many local chapters indicated a desire to get the league involved in energy issues at the national level. Thus, the May 1974 biennial convention of the league established an Energy Task Force within the Education Fund. The Energy Task Force is basically a study group having the purpose of informing the national staff and officers and the local membership about energy issues. The leaders of the league understand the uses of organizational structure for the achievement of desired ends, and this is evident in the structure of the task force. This group has its own, separate board of directors, which is organized in such a way that various points of view are certain to be presented to the task force staff. The task force board consists of thirty-five persons, twenty of whom are members of the board of directors of the league or of other divisions of the research operation of the Education Fund (for example, policy analysts in the fields of the environment, poverty, land use, and international relations), five of whom are league members with technical expertise relevant to energy issues, and ten of whom are representatives of different geographical regions of the United States (New England having different energy concerns from those of Texas, for example). This board of thirty-five meets every two months and reviews all the written work of the task force staff. This work must be approved by the task force board before it is sent out to the local chapters as study material, discussion guides, and so forth.

With a structure such as this, it is nearly impossible for the four-person staff of the Energy Task Force to prepare hasty and/or one-sided research reports. Officials of the league invariably speak the language of complexity, which is also used in publications of the league, when referring to energy issues. The following statement from a league discussion guide is typical:

> No easy choices lie ahead as the country attempts to fashion an energy policy. In the process of making energy decisions, difficult trade-offs will have to be made and conflicting public goals must be reconciled. The energy debate between the Administration and Congress—indeed throughout the nation —underlies this fact.[17]

---

[17] Isabelle Weber, *Citizens and Energy: The National Issues*, publication no. 5 of the League of Women Voters of the United States (Washington, D.C.: League of Women Voters, 1974), p. 1.

Given the complexity of energy issues and recognition of that complexity by the league, which even consciously embodies it within its organizational structure, it will take at least four years (from May 1974) for the league to arrive at a comprehensive statement on the question of energy. Indeed, members of the national staff are not sure that the league will be able to arrive at a comprehensive energy statement at all. But this is now the hope of the league. My view is that arriving at an overall position on energy will indeed be difficult for the league, but the league has managed to take stands on controversial positions in the past, as in supporting the Office of Economic Opportunity, the poverty agency; supporting land-use planning; supporting reciprocal-trade legislation in the late 1940s, when that was still a controversial subject; and calling for détente with China in the late 1960s. Thus the history of the league indicates that it can take controversial positions that must displease many of its members, at least at the beginning of the discussion and decision-making process. In the case of energy, arriving at a position on nuclear power will be the main stumbling block for the league, in my opinion.

Before May 1976, the league had adopted only a rather general statement on energy policy, which was drawn up by a special conference on energy with representatives from forty-eight states and which was then ratified by 848 of 901 local chapters that acted on the measure. This "energy conservation concurrence," as league parlance had it, enabled the organization to lobby in Washington in 1975. Upon this conservation platform, the Washington office lobbies for federal support of mass transit as a means of reducing gasoline consumption. The league follows other proposals for the conservation of energy—the requirement that appliance labels indicate the amount of energy that the appliances use, the adoption of federal building standards, the development of solar energy, the redesignation of rate structures—and will lobby for some of them.

At the biennial convention in May 1976, the sources of America's future energy supply was adopted as an official study topic. This means that local chapters are instructed to read and discuss materials on the various sources of energy and to reach conclusions about the issues involved by February 1978. If a consensus emerges about the resolution of such issues—including the development of nuclear power, the usefulness of coal, and so forth—the national organization will be able to go beyond its conservation position at the 1978 biennial convention.

The experience of other mass-membership public interest groups indicates that support for or opposition to nuclear electric power is at the heart of political conflict about energy, at least at present. The league is not at all close to taking a stand on nuclear energy, either pro or con. One staff member's impression is that antinuclear opinion in the league is stronger than pronuclear opinion. But the national staff is concerned that "some Leagues jump into opposition to nuclear without considering the consequences" (quotation from an interview). Two state chapters—those in Oregon and Wisconsin—have taken positions opposing the construction of more nuclear power plants. Two other state chapters—California and Arizona—have been much concerned about the issue but have been content to put out fact sheets giving arguments on both sides of the question. How the league handles the nuclear issue will determine whether it can arrive at a comprehensive position on energy or must content itself with partial statements.

Even if the league does not arrive at an overall energy position, however, it may be more important for the league to perform its function of stimulating and developing opinion on energy among the politically attentive public. If the league can mobilize itself on energy questions as it became mobilized on reciprocal trade in the early 1950s, the league will perform a major public service. The general public—even those members of it who are college graduates and are politically aware—does not seem to be well informed about energy problems. More public discussion of energy issues may be a prerequisite for congressional action in areas in which some people lose in the short run—increases in taxes on gasoline to conserve supplies, federal regulation of building codes for the sake of energy conservation, and so forth. The league has the capacity to contribute to the development of public opinion on energy. So far, its publications in the field of energy have been of high quality—informative and presenting various sides of an issue.[18]

In terms of our vocabulary of analysis, the league is a mass-membership organization that puts a particular emphasis on the communications function, defining that function largely in terms of research, study, and discussion in meetings at the local level. This type of communications activity is quite different from Nader's publicizing and persuasion. The emphasis placed by the league on political education stems from its organizational history, since the league was founded for the political education of newly enfranchised women voters in the 1920s.

With respect to energy, the league has not performed an initiatory function. It may yet perform an aggregative function, however, if

<hr>

[18] See, for example, the "Energy Fact Sheets: Energy 1–18," issued occasionally from February 1974 to September 1975 by the League of Women Voters Education Fund.

it is able to achieve agreement concerning the divisive issues having to do with energy. In particular, construction of nuclear power plants is the issue that is likely to be the stumbling block on the way to consensus. If the league is unable to take a position on nuclear power, it will have to content itself with a fragmentary position on energy.

If the league takes a comprehensive position, I expect that it will resemble the mixed-market position. On the one hand, the league is strongly committed to protection of the environment and does not shy away from governmental regulation, as in the case of its support for land-use planning.[19] On the other hand, the position of the league on energy will be moderated by its members who are independents or registered Republicans. Since the league makes decisions by consensus (their term for preponderant majorities of 90 percent or better), the more conservative members can veto radical aspects of the low-energy-growth position, such as dividing the oil companies. I think that the majority of the members of the league will be in favor of a moratorium on the construction of nuclear power plants once nuclear issues have been thoroughly debated (which will take another two years). But no one can say whether the nuclear moratorium will eventually gain adherence from the league, since the league does not take positions on issues concerning which a large proportion of its members are in opposition. One possible compromise might be opposition to construction of nuclear power plants except in areas in which there are strong economic arguments for generating electric power from nuclear sources, as there are in the New England states. If the league arrives at a moratorium position, it will find itself in another difficult situation—balancing environmental concerns with the consequent need to achieve a major rise in the production and use of coal for electric power.

The Sierra Club

The Sierra Club is a membership organization of conservationists and environmentalists which has 153,000 members, organized into 46 chapters (roughly corresponding to states) and 200 local groups. It is dedicated to the proposition "Not blind opposition to progress, but opposition to blind progress." "Wherever nature needs defense, the Sierra Club wants to be on the scene."[20] Members of the Sierra Club have done such an excellent job in their chosen task of defending

---

[19] *The National Voter*, vol. 25 (Summer 1975), pp. 6–7.

[20] These quotations, as well as the extensive quotation below, are taken from the leaflet "Why the Sierra Club?" (San Francisco: Sierra Club, n.d.).

the environment that they have become the most famous of the environmental lobbyists. This organization of dedicated conservationists is mobilized to offset "blind progress" in the sphere of energy development, but, as might be expected, it is not equipped to set forth a comprehensive statement concerning energy that would be at all likely to be adopted in the present era.

The history and the ambience of the Sierra Club are eloquently presented in a leaflet "Why the Sierra Club?", which wins the mythical "Thomas" (for Tom Paine) award as the best political pamphlet of 1975.

> "Something will have gone out of us as a people if we ever let the remaining wilderness be destroyed; if we permit the last virgin forests to be turned into comic books and plastic cigarette cases ..." Wallace Stegner's words express the same instinct that caused John Muir to found the Sierra Club in 1892. Muir knew that man's spirit can only survive in land that is spacious and unpolluted. John Muir founded the Sierra Club to enable more people to explore, enjoy and cherish the wildlands that are their heritage. . . . He wanted the Club to rescue these untrammelled places from those who see them only as wasted space. From experience, we know that these places are only as safe as people, knowing about them, want them to be. That is why we work to let more people know about them. . . .
>
> The Club helped bring the National Park Service and the Forest Service into existence; played a leading role in the establishment of such national parks as Kings Canyon, Olympic, Redwoods, and the North Cascades; was instrumental in creation of the Wilderness Preservation System and the Wild and Scenic Rivers System; and led the defense of Yosemite and Grand Canyon national parks and Dinosaur National Monument against dams. It has led efforts to obtain new parks in Alaska and to reform the Forest Service so as to curtail overcutting in national forests and to secure adequate study of roadless areas as potential wilderness.
>
> Protected areas must now be expanded: we need more national parks, wilderness areas, wild and scenic rivers, natural areas, and wildlife refuges; endangered species must be protected, estuaries safeguarded, scenic shorelines conserved, and open space reserved around our cities.
>
> The environment of the cities now also needs to be made fit for man: we must be more effective in combatting air and water pollution and the prevalence of chemical contaminants, noise, congestion and blight. Most of all, we

84

must prevent the exhaustion of resources and control the growth of human numbers so that a balance may be struck between man's works and the remaining natural world. Technology must be challenged to do a better job in managing the part of the planet it has already claimed. . . .

Wherever nature needs defense, the Sierra Club wants to be on the scene. We welcome all who want to be part of this defense. With new members strengthening its resources the Club can better act on behalf of all that is defenseless, irreplaceable and voiceless in our natural heritage.

Of the 153,000 persons who responded to the club's call to defend our natural heritage, about 78,000 reside in California, the state with which the club has historically been associated (it was named after the California mountain range). About 48,000 now reside east of the Mississippi, but the number of eastern and southern members of the club is growing steadily, as it takes on a national (as opposed to western) identity in response to the environmentalist movement of recent years.

The Sierra Club has particular influence with the forty-three-member California delegation, which constitutes 10 percent of the House of Representatives; the club has more members in California than has Common Cause. Most California congressmen want to stay on the right side of this organization of dedicated environmentalists, whose upper middle-class members are equipped with the skills in communication and research that make them influential in local politics. One congressman from the Los Angeles area pays as much attention to the Sierra Club as he does to any one of the leading economic interest groups of his district. By fortuitous accident, the San Francisco headquarters of the Sierra Club is in the district of Congressman Phillip Burton, who is emerging as one of the leading power brokers in the House and who is a leading environmentalist member of the House Interior Committee. Phil Burton appeared likely to rise to a high position in the Democratic leadership, as either speaker or majority leader, or, failing that, he was expected to become the chairman of the Interior Committee if Morris Udall gave up his House seat in quest of greater things. The Sierra Club could therefore greatly increase its lobbying effectiveness by working with Burton. To put things in their proper proportion, however, it must be noted that members of the Sierra Club are not yet numerous in most congressional districts outside of the West.

The Sierra Club is unified around the goals of environmentalism. These represent its first lobbying priority. Energy issues are a secondary priority, although of course environmental and energy issues overlap more often than not. But the club's dedication to environmentalist goals has an important effect—it is not possible for the club to put forth a comprehensive statement concerning energy that would appeal to a majority of congressmen in the world of present-day politics. The club is adamant in defending environmentalist goals, and it has opposed the development of nuclear power since January 1974. It backs stringent conservation measures, of course, and aggressive development of alternative sources of energy. But in my opinion, this is not an adequate program for dealing with the actual patterns of energy use in the United States during the next ten to fifteen years.

Thus, the Sierra Club puts forth a low-energy-growth position. It is doubtful that officials of the club could bring themselves to adopt the mixed-market-plus-coal position, since the club itself has been active in fighting strip mining, ideally seeking its abolition altogether. In an important environmental suit, moreover, the Sierra Club Legal Defense Fund fought the development of the Wyoming-Montana coal fields by going to court to require that interstate environmental-impact statements, rather than just local ones, be filed before the Interior Department is allowed to grant strip-mining permits on 478,000 acres of coal lands. This suit was successful at the appellate level, but was rejected by the Supreme Court in June 1976.[21] Some of the club's literature makes positive references to the possibilities for increasing production of coal through deep-mining methods, but it is unlikely that deep mining has the potential for taking up the slack in production that there would be if a nuclear moratorium went into effect and if strict environmental controls were placed upon domestic production of oil and coal.

In the light of this organization's history and values, however, it is not possible for the club's leaders to advocate strip mining of western coal or anything other than very strict controls on the development of offshore oil. If a member of the staff or the board came to such conclusions (which is extremely unlikely), he would feel compelled to resign from his position. There is only a minuscule chance that a group of the club's leaders might come to the conclusion that aggressive development of coal and/or oil is necessary. This possibility is as unlikely as that of a Republican presidential candidate suddenly advocating socialism.

For several years, many club members hoped that nuclear power would take up the slack if environmental controls put a ceiling on production of coal and oil. Other members opposed the development of nuclear power for the usual reasons, however. Debate waxed and

---

[21] Ben A. Franklin, "High Court Ruling to Ease Strip Mining of U.S. Coal," *New York Times*, June 29, 1976, p. 14.

waned for years, until in January 1974, the board of directors of the club passed a resolution in favor of a nuclear moratorium by a vote of 9-4-1. The resolution states that "the Sierra Club opposes the licensing, construction and operation of *new* nuclear reactors pending . . . resolution of the significant safety problems inherent in reactor operation, disposal of spent fuel, and possible diversion of nuclear material capable of use in weapons manufacture." The 1974 election of board members featured candidates who were in favor of nuclear power and candidates who were opposed to it; after the antinuclear faction had won most of the seats, the debate was considered resolved.[22]

One aspect of the structure of the Sierra Club is interesting, for it contains a prospect for conflict not found in such public interest organizations as Common Cause and Public Citizen, Inc. It was noted in the first chapter that joining the Sierra Club is economically beneficial to the outdoorsman. Thus, for dues of $15 a year, the member receives a monthly magazine and the opportunity to purchase at a discount a variety of books published by the club, he can travel at reduced fare on trips sponsored by the club, and he has the opportunity to participate in the club's hikes, wilderness outings, whitewater trips, and so forth, plus the option of staying in club lodges with sleeping accommodations. In addition, he gets the opportunity to meet others with outdoor interests at local Sierra Club meetings. Young persons looking for mates have been known to join the Sierra Club. Club membership is thus a bargain for a middle-income person with interests in the outdoors. Accordingly, while club members can be counted on to support environmentalist goals, there is otherwise enough diversity among them that conflict can develop over ambiguous issues such as the development of nuclear power. In particular, club membership brings enough economic benefits, and even social benefits, that members who disagree with the majority of the leaders of the club on some issue may remain and fight the issue, rather than simply quit the organization. This is a different situation from that of the Common Cause member, for example, who joins for ideological reasons and who will quit Common Cause if he does not like what Gardner is doing. (Consequently, members of Common Cause have been united to a remarkable degree in support of structure and process reforms, because members who did not like this policy have already quit.) Sierra Club members who may be disgruntled at the organization's political stands still have an incentive to stay in the

---

[22] For an excellent statement of the nuclear power position of the Sierra Club see "The Sierra Club and Nuclear Power" (San Francisco: Sierra Club, June 1975).

organization and fight. This is potentially an important distinction between public interest groups. Groups which offer economic and social incentives to join, rather than just ideological or solidaristic incentives, may have occasional bitter conflicts, because members who do not like the group's political stands will nevertheless stay in the organization.[23]

The Sierra Club departs from the low-energy-growth position in the matters of deregulation of the prices of oil and gas and reorganization of the oil industry. In such matters the club takes no position. Members of the staff report that there is a division of opinion among club members on the issue of government regulation versus market mechanisms in regard to setting oil and gas prices. This is not surprising. There is no reason to suspect that conservationists have a unified opinion on such matters, and in the absence of such unity, the club cannot take stands on potentially divisive issues which are of secondary priority.

In summary, on energy issues the Sierra Club has three major lobbying priorities: conservation of energy, strict protection of the natural environment, and countering proposals for speedy development of energy in the interest of assessing the impact on the environment. The Sierra Club supports the moratorium on development of nuclear power. It is against the strip mining of coal. It favors restriction of offshore oil development in the interest of protection of the environment. It does not now take stands on questions of energy pricing and of the corporate structure of the oil industry.

The Sierra Club is organized in such a way that it can perform an initiatory function in measures for the conservation of energy. There is unity of opinion among club members about energy conservation, which facilitates club action on such questions. Members of the staff and the board of the Sierra Club have more ideas about conservation of energy than do any of the other six organizations treated herein. The club appears to be one of the prime initiators of policy in the field of energy conservation when all of our national institutions are considered. Examples of club ideas are cited in Appendix E.

In the terms of our vocabulary of analysis, the Sierra Club is a mass-membership organization formed around the central value of conserving the natural environment. As such, it is well suited to initiate policy with respect to the conservation of energy. It is *not* suited for the formation of a comprehensive energy platform that fits the present-day world of politics, because the dedication of club members to environmentalism precludes aggregation and balancing of

---

[23] The generic statement of this type of idea is that of Albert O. Hirschman in *Exit, Voice, and Loyalty* (Cambridge, Mass: Harvard University Press, 1970).

interests that would appeal to a wider public. The club thus does not perform an aggregative function with respect to energy. Because of its environmentalism, the club tends toward the low-energy-growth position but it does not pursue the price regulation and corporate reorganization aspects of that position because of the diversity of opinion on such matters among its members. The club differs from other public interest groups (except for Consumers Union) in that it is economically beneficial for many persons to belong to the club. Thus the membership of the club will probably continue to increase and to retain a measure of diversity of political opinion. This means that the potential for divisive conflict within the club will increase also.

To give the flavor of the club's environmentalism I have included a compilation of actions taken by its board of directors in January 1974 on energy matters (Appendix D). As far as I know, these proposed policies have become club policy, although there may be differences in detail. Appendix E contains twenty proposals for action on energy conservation excerpted from the minutes of the energy committee of the board of directors.

Consumers Union

Founded in 1936, Consumers Union is an independent product-testing organization, which publishes *Consumer Reports,* a journal that the reader probably knows. CU derives almost all of its income from the 1.8 million subscriptions to *Consumer Reports,* plus newsstand sales and television rights (a syndicated CU series appears on fifty TV stations). In its fiscal year 1974–75, CU received a $140,000 grant from the Consumer Product Safety Commission to develop a proposed safety standard for power lawn mowers. But the main revenues of Consumers Union during this period were $15.8 million received from sales of *Consumer Reports* and its TV series. Ninety-nine percent of this $16 million budget is devoted to product testing, publishing, and membership maintenance. During the fiscal year 1974–75, however, $151,794 was spent for "advocacy," although this amount was apparently decreased to $115,000 for 1975–76.[24] Consumers Union maintains a Washington office with three lawyer advocates for consumer interests, and it also maintains a lawyer in California. This budget makes the basic commitment of Consumers Union quite clear.

CU's organizational definition as a product-testing organization, as opposed to a consumer advocacy organization, was evident when Ralph Nader resigned from the board of directors of CU on October

---

[24] *Consumer Reports,* vol. 40 (October 1975), pp. 634–35.

1, 1975, after he had served for eight years in that capacity. In his letter of resignation, Nader stated:

> I can better use the ten days a year, which would be spent on CU matters, in other pursuits within the consumer movement more broadly defined.
>
> My principal interests on the Board have been to help CU realize more of its potential in the area of consumer investigation, advocacy and organization. . . . There is a division of philosophy on the Board as to how much energy and resources are to be directed toward changing major consumer injustices through consumer action instead of just informing some consumers about some of them.
>
> While CU has stepped up its advocacy effort in the Washington and California offices and has included more investigative reporting in *Consumer Reports,* its overwhelming effort is in testing and communicating the results about products. Neither the majority of the Board, nor most of the upper management nor the employees union leadership wants to urge or see the fundamental changes needed to make a truly Consumers Union of power, presence, and priority.[25]

In responding to Nader's letter, CU Executive Director Rhoda H. Karpatkin noted that he "raises yet again a question debated throughout our history" and agreed with Nader's picture of the CU organization, although, of course, her tone was different.

> There is little disagreement anywhere within CU that, great as is the need to strengthen consumer advocacy in the courts, before government agencies, and in the marketplace, CU's contribution must be ancillary to, not at the expense of an impartial product-testing and reporting program. For the latter is CU's unique contribution to the consumer interest.[26]

Theoretically one might expect that a consumers' union with a budget of $16 million would be the dominant public interest group in advocating energy policy, but its energy advocacy is in fact limited to the efforts of one person, lawyer Peter Schuck, who is the director of the Washington office of CU. As Schuck stated in an interview, he does not have enough time even to read all of the hearing notices and opinions of the important energy-related agencies, the Federal Energy Administration and the Federal Power Commission.

Another factor limits the political activity of Consumers Union—the postal regulations. CU is permitted by the Internal Revenue Code

---

[25] *Consumer Reports,* vol. 40 (September 1975), p. 525.

[26] Ibid., p. 524.

to lobby with respect to measures calling for action by Congress, but Schuck and his colleagues do not lobby in the direct sense of going "up to the Hill" and attempting to persuade congressmen. If they did so, they fear that the postal authorities would change their mailing status, thereby raising considerably the expenses of an organization that mails 1.8 million magazines a month. Representatives of CU are invited to testify before Congress about once a month, however. CU personnel probably have informal contacts with congressional staff, but I did not ask the question for fear that some postal authority would read this monograph!

There is an organizational wisdom in the avoidance by CU of a large amount of political activity. Just as it can be economically beneficial for the outdoorsman to join the Sierra Club, so it is usually economically beneficial for a person having an upper middle-class income to pay $11 for a subscription to *Consumer Reports*. Subscribers become members of Consumers Union simply by virtue of taking the trouble to vote by mail ballot in the annual CU election. The 1.8 million CU subscribers hold diverse political opinions, and numerous stands that might be taken by CU on political issues would conflict with opinions strongly held by many subscribers. Rather than quit, however, those subscribers might retain their subscription and fight— by voting for a slate of "outs" which could surely appear in such circumstances, for example. Political infighting would lower the morale and efficiency of this now effective product-testing organization. In addition, more subscribers, irritated at such hypothetical political stands, might cancel their subscriptions and drop out of the organization. This would substantially reduce the funds available for product testing. (The more items CU includes in its testing samples, the more reliable are its results, but such reliability is expensive.) There are thus sound organizational reasons for Consumers Union to avoid taking a great many political stands.

Severe financial problems have been another factor limiting the political activities of CU in recent years. CU ran a deficit of $3,051,306 during its fiscal year 1974–75, when its income was $16,064,373.[27] This financial disaster was the result of an increase in the price of newsprint and a sudden drop in the number of subscribers, down from 2.25 million to 1.8 million between 1973 and 1975. Most public interest groups suffered a drop in membership during that period, but CU also raised its subscription rates from $8 to $11 and was surprised at the number of subscribers who did not renew.

In spite of all these difficulties, however, Consumers Union has

[27] *Consumer Reports*, vol. 40 (October 1975), p. 635.

been able to initiate important lawsuits having to do with the pricing of oil and gas. Mr. Schuck regards three lawsuits filed by CU as having a potentially important impact on energy policy. In 1974 Schuck won a suit which challenged an FEA ruling that allowed the prices of unleaded gasoline to be set at the same level as the prices of premium gasoline, even though unleaded gasoline costs no more to refine than so-called regular gasoline. The FEA eventually admitted to having violated its own procedures in this ruling. This action saved consumers perhaps $200 million.[28] Consumers Union has not had equivalent success in its other two major energy lawsuits. One action challenged the FEA's interpretation of the Emergency Petroleum Allocation Act and alleged that prices on "new oil" had to be controlled under the act. This case was lost in the appellate court by a vote of 4-3. The third suit, challenging a 1972 ruling of the Federal Power Commission (FPC) that allowed the raising of prices on Southern Louisiana natural gas from twenty-six cents per thousand cubic feet to forty-five cents, alleged procedural irregularities by the FPC; this suit has been meandering through the courts and the FPC for more than three years. Since 1972, however, the average interstate price of FPC-regulated "new" gas has risen to fifty-two cents (January 1976), which means that even if CU won its suit, gas producers would *now* get forty-five cents per thousand cubic feet anyway. The gas fields in question are second in size only to the Alaskan fields, so this esoteric matter of pricing involves billions of dollars.

In terms of our vocabulary, Consumers Union specializes in energy lawsuits involving the pricing of oil and gas, although it is occasionally involved in other energy matters (invited testimony regarding consumer participation in the FEA, for example). CU thus performs a limited, but significant, initiatory function in challenging rulings of the FPC and the FEA. CU does not perform major communications or aggregative functions with respect to energy.

Consumers Union is a mass-membership organization, united around the central values of the testing of products and the dissemination of product information. A wide-ranging advocacy effort with respect to energy would provoke conflict among the members of CU; such a course of action is therefore not pursued. If CU should solve its present financial problems and consequently be able to expand its advocacy effort, its additional efforts would be channeled into types of consumer advocacy that would not be controversial among its subscribers. If CU were to expand its advocacy efforts with respect to energy, the expansion would probably occur within its pres-

---

[28] Theoretically speaking, however, lowering the price would reduce the supply of unleaded gas available to the public.

ent area of action—lawsuits challenging increases in the prices of oil and gas—plus areas such as promoting measures having to do with the conservation of energy, alternative sources of energy, and participation by consumers within the structures of energy agencies. Such activities would be acceptable to nearly everyone within the CU organization. In conclusion, while Consumers Union is a public interest organization with a budget of $16 million, the main priority of the organization is product testing and consumer information. CU is unlikely to develop a controversial, wide-ranging advocacy program with respect to energy.

Consumer Federation of America: Energy Policy Task Force

The Consumer Federation of America was established in 1968 as a confederation of 140 groups interested in promoting consumer advocacy within our national political institutions.[29] CFA acts as the Washington representative of its member organizations, keeping them informed about the progress of bills. It issues pamphlets about such matters as the pricing of prescription drugs, life insurance, pricing practices of supermarkets, and the voting records of congressmen on consumer issues. It sponsors small research projects through its Paul Douglas Consumer Research Center (a separate organization for tax purposes). CFA maintains a staff of about ten persons, including volunteers, and has four lobbyists, including its energy lobbyists—Lee C. White and Ellen Berman. It thus makes a modest but active lobbying effort. There are now about 200 member organizations within the federation—150 local organizations such as local consumer action units, public power companies, and rural electric cooperatives—plus 50 national organizations, most of them national labor unions. Other national organizations within CFA are national consumer groups (including Consumers Union) and federations of public power companies and rural electric co-ops. The 200 groups hold a yearly assembly which serves as a three-day national convention of the consumer movement.

The management of publicly owned power companies and of rural electric cooperatives became conscious of possible energy shortages before the general public became aware of the problem. Informal discussions among members of the board of CFA about energy questions during 1972 led to the formation of the CFA Energy Policy Task Force, which was launched in March 1973 before the OPEC price increase. Twenty of the constituent organizations of CFA agreed to

[29] Mark V. Nadel, *The Politics of Consumer Protection* (Indianapolis: Bobbs-Merrill Company, 1971), p. 159.

support the energy task force with small donations, and the number of supporting organizations has since increased to thirty-five. Representatives of these thirty-five task force organizations constitute a separate board, which has met several times a year, when it has been necessary to make major decisions about the activities of the task force.

It is worthwhile to inspect the list of organizations that were members of the CFA Energy Policy Task Force in September 1975 (see Table 5). Fourteen of the constituent organizations are public power organizations or rural electric co-ops, thirteen others are associated with labor, and five are farm groups (which are not so numerous within the CFA as a whole). The influence of representatives of public power organizations and of labor on the board of the energy task force differentiates the CFA from most public interest groups that are concerned about energy. Public power companies and rural electric co-ops are greatly concerned that they receive sufficient energy to meet the needs of their customers. Some of their electricity is generated by nuclear power plants or by coal-fired plants. These public power companies do not want the CFA to take aggressive stands against nuclear power or for strict environmental constraints on the production of coal. In addition to this concern about the production of energy there is a built-in concern about jobs provided by the representatives of labor.

The CFA Energy Policy Task Force is therefore not active on issues concerned with nuclear power or coal. Its literature does not contain such heavy emphasis on environmentalism in discussing energy policy as does that of most public interest groups. Energy task force statements refer to the "need for development" of domestic oil and gas resources—another emphasis typically lacking in the statements of public interest groups. Reflecting the concerns of the public power companies, labor unions, and consumerists who make up the organization, the activity of the CFA task force is not so much in opposition to development as it is critical of corporate energy policies. Accordingly, the task force has been particularly active in support of the possible establishment of a federal oil and gas corporation, opposition to the deregulation of natural gas and petroleum, and opposition to appointing energy industry executives to federal policy-making positions, such as that of commissioner of the FPC.

The interests of the member organizations of the task force coincide with the need of the task force to specialize. Thus, the task force staff consists of only two persons—Lee C. White and Ellen Berman. A lawyer who also holds a degree in electrical engineering, Mr. White has been associated politically with the Kennedy family. He served on Senator John F. Kennedy's staff in the 1950s, served as

Table 5
MEMBER ORGANIZATIONS OF
CFA ENERGY POLICY TASK FORCE

Adams Electric Cooperative, Inc. (Pennsylvania)
AFL-CIO
Allegheny Electric Cooperative, Inc. (Pennsylvania)
American Federation of State, County and Municipal Employees,
   AFL-CIO
American Federation of Teachers, AFL-CIO
American Public Gas Association
American Public Power Association
Consumers Union
Cooperative League of the USA
Industrial Union Department, AFL-CIO
International Association of Machinists and Aerospace Workers,
   AFL-CIO
International Brotherhood of Electrical Workers, AFL-CIO
Kansas Municipal Utilities
Lincoln (Nebraska) Electric System
Maritime Trades Department, AFL-CIO
Minnesota Farmers Union
National Farmers Organization
National Farmers Union
National Rural Electric Cooperation Association
North Dakota Farmers Union
Northeast Missouri Electric Power Cooperative
Northeast Public Power Association
Northwest Public Power Association
Oil, Chemical and Atomic Workers International Union, AFL-CIO
Pennsylvania Rural Electric Association
Service Employees International Union, AFL-CIO
South Dakota Farmers Union
Tennessee Valley Public Power Association
Textile Workers Union of America, AFL-CIO
Tillamook Peoples Utility District (Oregon)
United Auto Workers
United States Conference of Mayors
United Steelworkers of America, AFL-CIO
Washington Public Utility Districts' Association
Wisconsin State AFL-CIO

Source: Consumer Federation of America, September 1975.

counsel to Presidents Kennedy and Johnson, was chairman of the
FPC from 1966 to 1969, and managed Sargent Shriver's vice-presidential campaign in 1972. White is chairman of the task force, but he
serves as a volunteer, deriving his income from a Washington law
practice. Ms. Berman is the sole day-to-day staff member of the task
force, performing all the duties of a Washington representative—

lobbying, communicating with member organizations, doing research, issuing press releases, tracing the progress of legislation and of lawsuits, and raising money. The fact that White has been conversant with energy problems for at least a decade has enabled him to hasten the decision-making process followed by public interest groups that faced energy questions for the first time in 1973. The CFA task force was thereby able to announce a fifteen-point program, involving some technical matters, immediately after the group's inception in March 1973 (see below). Nevertheless, expanding the task force purview to include activity on nuclear, coal, and complex environmental matters would severely strain its two-person staff.[30]

The fifteen-point program of the energy task force, as set forth in its initial press release, dated March 26, 1973, reads as follows:

> White said that the Task Force will work to implement the following goals:
>
> Promotion and implementation of energy-conserving measures and of the wise and efficient use of energy;
>
> Consolidation within the Federal Government of responsibilities in the field of energy policy and implementation;
>
> Vastly increased government expenditures for energy research and development;
>
> Tougher anti-trust enforcement to prevent monopoly of energy sources;
>
> Tighter controls over the development of publicly-owned fuel reserves;
>
> Formation of a Federal fuels corporation;
>
> Federal and state plant-siting programs for oil refineries and associated facilities;
>
> Extension of FPC authority to include intrastate as well as interstate sales of natural gas;
>
> Elimination or reduction of financial incentives to oil companies to explore for new oil and gas at the expense of domestic resources and development;
>
> Continuation of the 2 percent REA loan program for rural electric cooperatives serving sparsely settled areas and whose financial situation requires loans at 2 percent interest;
>
> Retention of Federal control over the well-head price of natural gas;

---

[30] Berman stated that she expected the task force to become active on coal policies as these become increasingly important. However, we still expect that the task force organizations would have a difficult time agreeing on a position on strip mining, for example. CFA might be able to act in regard to the leasing of coal lands to oil companies, though, as this would be congruent with the critical view of oil companies held by most of the member organizations.

Elimination of the oil import quota system to be replaced by a tariff system if necessary;

Federal regulation that will have as a primary objective consumer protection;

Appointment of consumer-oriented members to Federal regulatory agencies;

Establishment of consumers counsels.

White said that while all of the supporting groups may not "necessarily subscribe to each of the specific positions enunciated by the Task Force," there was "complete agreement" on the basic thrusts of the Task Force goals.[31]

The reader will note that this initial platform emphasizes federal activity with respect to oil and gas. Oil import quotas were abolished by President Nixon in 1973; the Federal Energy Administration was created after the time of this press release to centralize the handling of energy questions. Even so, this initial statement serves to indicate the basic direction that the Energy Policy Task Force has followed since 1973. (A longer description of these points is contained in Appendix F, below.)

Lee White and the task force have performed a policy-initiatory function in advocating the establishment of a federal oil and gas corporation, an idea which now has widespread support but which has been associated particularly with the CFA. This publicly owned corporation is envisioned as a sort of TVA for the oil and gas industry. It is an idea which can command the united support of the public power, electric co-op, labor, liberal farm, and consumer constituent organizations of the task force. While this idea has doubtless been promulgated by various persons since the 1890s, I use the term *policy initiation* to refer to the active injection of an idea onto the agenda of Washington decision makers—something that Lee White has been doing in recent years. In 1974 he described the idea as follows:

A Federal Oil and Gas Corp., as proposed in pending legislation, would:

—Explore for and develop petroleum resources to meet national needs, not to maximize profits.

—Develop and use the most advanced methods to minimize damage to the environment in all phases of the petroleum process.

—Provide for the first time in our history, complete and accurate information for public and government on the costs of producing oil and gas, as well as other data on the petroleum business.

---

[31] "Purpose and Policies: Energy Policy Task Force, Consumer Federation of America" (Washington, D.C.: CFA Energy Policy Task Force, 1973).

—Manage discovered reserves to reduce U.S. reliance on foreign petroleum sources.

—Sell petroleum in a way that insures that a fair share goes to independent refiners and distributors, thus promoting a truly competitive industry.

—Provide a competitive spur to the privately owned oil industry.

There was comparatively little need to consider major alternatives to our privately operated petroleum industry as long as the country's needs were being met. However, when things go wrong, as they obviously have recently, the system must be reexamined.

The advantages of a government oil corporation are many. Energy shortages may exist for decades. In this situation, there should be an energy-producing organization motivated not by profits, but by national needs. There is nothing inherently wrong with the profit incentive, but where the product is as essential to national well-being and security as energy, at least part of the country's effort to provide it ought to be motivated by America's security, and the needs of the public.[32]

The CFA Energy Policy Task Force is also quite active in opposing deregulation of the prices of oil and gas. When I interviewed Berman in early October 1975, she was working at a somewhat frantic pace in opposition to the Pearson-Bentsen gas deregulation measure which eventually passed the Senate that month.[33] Before the vote was taken to override President Ford's veto of the now forgotten Democratic energy bill of August 1975, the task force ran a striking two-page ad in the *Washington Post* entitled "Get mad, America. Get mad." The ad reflected the prevailing opinion that sustaining the veto (the eventual outcome) would lead to an immediate deregulation of domestic oil prices: "If Congress doesn't override the President's veto tomorrow, your family's fuel bill will go up $300 next year. And it will keep going up until you get mad!"[34] After the effort to override the veto failed to get the necessary two-thirds majority in the Senate, CFA ran a full-page ad in the *Post* listing the thirty-nine Ford supporters in large, quarter-inch letters.[35] The ad was headlined: "Now you know who to get mad at when your fuel bill goes up." Both ads

---

[32] Lee C. White, "A TVA-Type Competitor for Petroleum Industry," *Los Angeles Times*, February 3, 1975.

[33] *Congressional Quarterly*, vol. 33 (October 25, 1975), pp. 2292–95.

[34] *Washington Post*, September 9, 1975; see also *Congressional Quarterly*, vol. 33 (September 13, 1975), pp. 1940–41.

[35] *Washington Post*, September 14, 1975.

were signed by the "Energy Action Committee," identified as a group of sixteen persons prominent in the public interest movement, labor, and entertainment.[36]

The CFA task force sets forth only a fragment of an energy policy. It has well-developed ideas about government regulation of oil and gas and about a partial reorganization of the oil industry. It advocates conservation and has conducted some modest research towards that end.[37] CFA supports the development of alternative sources of energy. But a comprehensive energy policy cannot be presented without reference to nuclear power and coal, and CFA cannot do this because of differing opinions among its member organizations.

The CFA Energy Policy Task Force is able to initiate policies on the subject on which its staff and board are united—oil and gas policy and, in particular, the organization of a federal oil corporation. As stated earlier, CFA does not perform an aggregative function with respect to energy. It performs a minor communications function by informing the thirty-five constituent organizations of policy developments in Washington. The member organizations then have the option of trying to influence policy making.

The CFA Energy Policy Task Force cannot be described as either a staff group (because the board is important in limiting the range of positions) or as a membership group. It is interesting that the board of the task force represents a greater variety of interests than do the boards of membership groups discussed in this book. In some ways, this task force can be described as a permanent lobbying coalition in that it resembles the Washington lobbying coalitions formed in pursuit of a single objective, but the task force was formed in pursuit of a series of related objectives and is presumably a long-lasting organization.

---

[36] The Energy Action Committee was dormant for the following three months, but it suddenly appeared on the political scene in January 1976 with financing, vigorous direction, and skill in public relations. Of the sixteen signers of the original CFA ads, Harold Willens, Paul Newman (the movie actor), Miles Rubin, and Leo Wyler put up $600,000 to start a new public interest lobby to oppose the oil companies on energy matters. These four are all California liberals. They hired James Flug, formerly a legislative aide to Senator Edward Kennedy, as staff director. Plans are being made to solicit memberships through mass mailings. The founders of the EAC have chosen to oppose deregulation of natural gas and to support the division of the large oil companies and the founding of a federal energy corporation. In a sense, the Energy Action Committee is analogous to Americans for Energy Independence. Thus, as Americans for Energy Independence is coalescing around the development-independence values of its founders, so EAC will form around the platform of its founders' opposition to the oil corporations.

[37] See Jeff Bander et al., *Energy Conservation in Buildings: New Roles for Cities and Citizen Groups*, published by the National League of Cities and the United States Conference of Mayors in cooperation with the Energy Policy Task Force of the Consumer Federation of America, January 1975.

Americans for Energy Independence

Americans for Energy Independence is the result of an effort to form a public interest group representing the development-and-independence position. This organization is still in the process of formation, so one cannot be sure of the form that it will eventually take, and, indeed, one cannot be sure whether Americans for Energy Independence will continue in existence. At the least, however, Americans for Energy Independence represents an interesting attempt to influence the politics of energy, while it has the potential to be influential.

Americans for Energy Independence is committed to pressing for the development of domestic sources of energy, particularly nuclear power and coal, to achieve the goal of independence of OPEC exporters. This organization is also interested in public education— convincing the public that there is indeed an energy crisis—and in promoting energy conservation measures. So far Americans for Energy Independence exists for the purposes of policy research and public education. It is not officially a lobbying organization, which means that it cannot approach members of Congress concerning legislation. (It thus can receive tax-deductible donations.) Some of the leaders of Americans for Energy Independence would like to take on lobbying status, however, and thus the organization may change its character in the near future.

Americans for Energy Independence was established between March and June 1975 by a group of persons particularly concerned about America's need to develop its own sources of energy for the sake of our foreign policy, our standard of living, and the maintenance of jobs. Prominent in the founding of the organization were Hans Bethe, a nuclear physicist at Cornell University and a leading defender of nuclear energy, Zalman Shapiro, manager of the Fusion Power Systems division of Westinghouse Electric, I. W. Abel, president of the United Steelworkers of America, and Endicott Peabody, governor of Massachusetts from 1965 to 1967, Democratic vice-presidential aspirant in 1972, and now a Washington lawyer. These persons assembled a prestigious board, including representatives of energy-related industries, labor, science, and religion (see Table 6 for a list of the officers and members of the board). The board met for the first time in June 1975 and appointed Elmo Zumwalt, former chief of naval operations, to be president of the new organization. In an action which brought Americans for Energy Independence its greatest publicity during the first few months of its existence, however, Zumwalt resigned in September after the executive board voted not to accept the former admiral's choice of an executive director. Lane Kirk-

Table 6
OFFICIALS OF AMERICANS FOR ENERGY INDEPENDENCE,
DECEMBER 1975

OFFICERS

Chairman of the Board	Professor Hans Bethe
Vice Chairman of the Board	Mr. Joseph Keenan
Vice Chairman of the Board	Mr. Robert Nathan
Acting President	Gov. Endicott Peabody
Secretary	Gov. Endicott Peabody
Treasurer	Harold Greenwald, Esq.
Chairman of the Executive Committee	Dr. Zalman Shapiro

BOARD OF DIRECTORS

Mr. I. W. Abel, President,
United Steelworkers of
America

Professor Hans A. Bethe
Nobel Laureate,
Cornell University

Right Reverend John H. Burt
Bishop of Ohio (Episcopal)

Mr. Jose A. Cabranes
Legal Advisor to Yale
University

Dr. Richard M. Cyert, President,
Carnegie-Mellon University

Ms. Evelyn Dubrow, Legislative
Director, International
Ladies Garment Workers
Union

Mr. James Finn
Editor, *Worldview*

Harold Greenwald, Esq.
Greenwald, Kovner and
Goldsmith

Ms. Dorothy I. Height
National President, National
Council of Negro Women

Dr. Dixy Lee Ray, Former
Chairman, Atomic Energy
Commission

Professor Robert Hofstadter
Nobel Laureate,
Stanford University

Mr. Joseph D. Keenan
International Secretary
International Brotherhood of
Electrical Workers

Mr. Philip M. Klutznick, Chairman,
Research & Policy Committee
of the Committee for Economic
Development

Mr. Louis Martin, Vice President,
Sengstacke Newspapers

Professor Hans J. Morgenthau,
New School for Social Studies

Mr. Robert R. Nathan
Consulting Economist

Endicott Peabody, Esq.
Former Governor of
Massachusetts

Mrs. Esther Peterson, Vice
President, Giant Food

Mr. Jim Ramey, Vice President,
Stone & Webster Engineering
Corp.

Mr. Bayard Rustin, President,
A. Philip Randolph Institute

Leonard Sagan, M.D.
Stanford University

Dr. Cecily Cannan Selby
Former Executive Director,
Girl Scouts of America

Mr. John Schiff
Kuhn, Loeb & Company

Dr. Zalman M. Shapiro, Manager,
Fusion Power Systems,
Westinghouse Electric Corp.

Dr. Joseph Sternstein (Rabbi)
Temple Beth Shalom,
New Jersey

Mr. William E. Towell
Exec. Vice President, American
Forestry Association

Source: Americans for Energy Independence.

101

land, secretary-treasurer of the AFL-CIO, resigned from the executive board in support of Zumwalt. About half of the twelve-member staff also resigned in support of Zumwalt. For two or three weeks, the continued existence of Americans for Energy Independence was in doubt, but the organization survived and has shown that it has a considerable base of resources. A replacement for Zumwalt was not easily found, for the president, as the major spokesman of a group, has a critical part in shaping its public image, but five months later, in February 1976, Dr. Cecily Cannan Selby, formerly national executive director of the Girl Scouts of America, was appointed president of Americans for Energy Independence.

The reasons for Zumwalt's resignation are unclear. Americans for Energy Independence staffers say that their board did not accept Zumwalt's choice of a staff director because the candidate, a former naval officer, was not an energy expert. (The job included the preparation of policy research papers on energy.) A writer for *Science* magazine thought that Zumwalt was forced out by Zalman Shapiro for being insufficiently enthusiastic about nuclear power.[38] Furthermore Zumwalt at this time seemed to be campaigning for the Democratic nomination for senator from Virginia, a peculiar situation for the major spokesman of a purported public interest group to be in. In retrospect it seems that Zumwalt did not fit in with the group of original organizers in a number of respects. He may have been hired in haste in the attempt to get the organization moving.

Americans for Energy Independence raised $600,000 in organizational costs during its first year of operation. Although its funds came initially from electric utilities and the electrical equipment industry (Westinghouse and General Electric), Americans for Energy Independence did not try to conceal its search for funds from other energy-related industries, such as coal, gas pipelines, and the paper and pulp industry (dependent on imported oil for drying operations).

Americans for Energy Independence had hoped at first to get major support from membership contributions of $10 a person from the general public. By the spring of 1976, however, this expectation had been dropped because of the infeasibility of getting enough members through recruitment at meetings sponsored by the organization or through internal communications within energy-related businesses. Americans for Energy Independence did not try to get members through a mass mailing, for reasons that I would surmise to have included expense (now about twenty cents a letter including the cost of renting a list of names) plus initial uncertainty as to which lists to

---

[38] Deborah Shapley, "Americans for Energy Independence: Independence from Whom?" *Science*, vol. 190 (October 3, 1975), pp. 31–32.

rent. Unlike the situation of those who would organize ideologically liberal, radical, or conservative organizations, or even those who would form environmentalist, good-government, or consumer organizations, it is not clear where Americans for Energy Independence could obtain mailing lists with good cost-benefit ratios for attracting members. Furthermore, 1975–76 was not a good time (in comparison to the years 1970–73) to start a mass-membership organization because of the squeeze on the budgets of upper middle-class families.

What sort of a group is Americans for Energy Independence? Can we call it a public interest group, according to the definition set forth in Chapter 2? The elements of the definition are a public interest group seeks to represent the interests of the whole public; it does not chiefly represent some specific economic interest; and it is not one of a list of traditional types of interest groups. At present Americans for Energy Independence is a mixed bag in terms of these three criteria. First, it seeks to represent the whole public; second, it is closely tied to the energy industry at this time, particularly to nuclear power and electric utilities; third, it is not a traditional type of interest group. I think most persons would agree that Americans for Energy Independence would become more like a public interest group the more it departed from financial dependence on energy-related industries and substituted dependence on contributions from a variety of sources, particularly if such contributions came primarily from persons working *outside* energy-related industries and if such contributions were to become nationwide rather than regional (concentrated in New England, for example).

At present a coalition representing electric utilities, General Electric and Westinghouse, the Steelworkers, the Electrical Workers and other unions, scientists, persons particularly concerned with foreign policy questions (Hans Morgenthau), and New Englanders is to be found among staff, directors, and contributors. One of the two staff members whom I interviewed, John Gordon, was an electrical engineer working in the nuclear division of Westinghouse who had been lent to Americans for Energy Independence (which eventually paid his salary). After Zumwalt's resignation, rapid action by I. W. Abel, president of the United Steelworkers of America, in lending staff assistance to replace the Zumwalt coterie was very helpful in maintaining the organization. At the same time, Joseph Keenan of the Electrical Workers helped Americans for Energy Independence by providing organizational and management services—in aid of an attempt to recruit members in New England, for example.

As of May 1976, Americans for Energy Independence had not issued any official policy papers, but the general direction of the organization was clear in the statements of former Acting President Endicott Peabody, which surely reflected the opinions of all those active in the organization. As noted, the dominant theme in the statements of Americans for Energy Independence has been the critical need to develop domestic sources of energy in *the short run*. Leaders of Americans for Energy Independence see such development as vital to the maintenance of prosperity and jobs, and therefore vital for the maintenance of a stable society. Americans for Energy Independence is critical of those who emphasize the development of alternative sources of energy, such as solar power, viewing their position as an intellectual evasion of a confrontation with America's short-term crisis in energy supply. Americans for Energy Independence clearly believes that aggressive environmentalism hurts the national welfare by restricting the production of energy. Americans for Energy Independence also believes that the developing of Alaskan oil and offshore oil and strip mining of western coal are necessary. Former Acting President Peabody stated that nuclear power is safe with the type of safeguards which we have at the moment.[39] Consequently, he favors further development of the nuclear alternative.

Americans for Energy Independence stresses issues having to do with nuclear power and coal in its current statements. I expect that this group will defend nuclear power and the strip mining of western coal in the big political fights now emerging. It is interesting that Americans for Energy Independence has kept its distance from the oil industry. The oil and gas industry is little represented on the board or staff or among its contributors. I surmise that the founders of Americans for Energy Independence made the decision to stay away from issues having to do with oil and gas, because of the current unpopularity of the oil industry and because oil and gas development positions are well covered by such lobbies as the large American Petroleum Institute. In my judgment, this is good political reasoning. Americans for Energy Independence will gain more support by emphasizing nuclear power and coal.

Americans for Energy Independence is also concerned that the public be convinced of the reality of the energy crisis and of a consequent need for determined policy making or even for national emergency measures with respect to energy. Americans for Energy Independence also, with apparent sincerity, stresses the need for

---

[39] Endicott Peabody, "Nuclear Energy's Role in Meeting the American Energy Crisis" (Arlington, Va.: Americans for Energy Independence, 1975). This is testimony given November 14, 1975, at the New England regional hearing of the Energy and Environment Subcommittee of the Committee on Interior and Insular Affairs, U.S. House of Representatives.

conservation of energy. Another goal of the organization is to provoke more action from the government with respect to conservation.

In terms of our vocabulary, Americans for Energy Independence is a staff organization (with about five quite active board members), formed around the values of the development-and-independence position. It hopes to issue a series of policy papers during 1976–77 which together would form a comprehensive platform for energy development and independence. It is thus attempting to perform an aggregative function in setting forth a development-independence position. It also hopes to perform a communications function by giving its policy statements wide public currency. Whether it will succeed in doing so cannot now be determined. This organization has no plans at present to perform an initiatory function with respect to energy.

In conclusion, Americans for Energy Independence is an unusual coalition of various groups and persons concerned about the need to develop domestic sources of energy. It might become a public interest group, as defined earlier, if it should recruit a variety of geographically dispersed contributors who are not concentrated in the energy industry. On the other hand, Americans for Energy Independence might continue its present dependence on energy-related industries for funds and manpower and therefore would not ordinarily be termed a public interest group.

6
CONCLUSIONS

Public interest groups appear to have a significant impact on the process of making policy with respect to energy.[1] I have presented a sufficient variety of information about seven public interest lobbies to enable the reader to make up his own mind about the desirability of their activities. The reader's evaluation of public interest groups will depend partly on his or her own opinions about energy policies such as the development of nuclear power, conservation, deregulation of natural gas, the structure of the oil industry, strip mining and other issues having to do with the production of coal, the development of offshore oil, the relative significance of environmental values, and so forth.

This volume is not the definitive work on public interest groups or even on the decision making of public interest groups on questions related to energy. There is a need for more scholarly research on the subject of public interest groups and energy. Such research might cover the environmentalist groups that I have omitted and might explore the processes of the handling of technical information by nonexperts. Another type of research that is needed is case studies of the making of policy with respect to energy, which could establish the extent of the power exercised by public interest groups with respect to this matter.

---

[1] For example, public interest groups have influenced energy policy by delaying the construction of the Alaska pipeline, by speeding up the process of holding state-by-state referendums on the construction of nuclear power plants, by lobbying for strip-mining control legislation, by filing lawsuits which slowed down the mining of Wyoming-Montana coal and the development of offshore oil fields, and by lobbying for the development of solar power and other alternative sources of energy.

Conclusions about Public Interest Groups

Here are some conclusions about public interest groups in concise form.

1. Public interest lobbies will continue to be influential in the short-run future (five years or so). Their mass support is derived largely from college-educated, middle-class persons with skeptical attitudes about the present quality of American government, a type of opinion which shows no signs of immediate decline.

2. Leaders and followers of public interest groups view politics according to the civic-balance system of beliefs—the belief that many policies are controlled by special interests and that the function of public interest groups is to counteract the power of special interests for the benefit of the public at large.

3. Public interest group leaders in Washington attempt reform through the politics of ad hoc coalitions (including public interest lawsuits) specific to particular policies and issues. They do not expect to achieve reform through scientific, impartial public administration (the Progressive idea), nor do they expect to reform society through the actions of a unified federal executive branch (the goal of the New Deal).

4. *The Logic of Collective Action* by Mancur Olson, Jr., provides a rationale for the need for public interest groups to represent public interests that are widespread but difficult to organize within a pluralist democracy. (Note that this is different from discussing *the* public interest.)

5. There may be several different public interests, sometimes on various sides of a question, as well as numerous types of special interests involved in actual policy-making situations such as those having to do with energy.

6. Public interest groups usually do not represent *all* the public interests that are related to any given policy situation.

7. Organizational characteristics, such as the nature of the supporting coalition or the past activities of the organization, constrain the choices of a public interest lobby as to which public interests to represent.

8. Public interest groups typically operate by consensus (or near consensus) in deciding their positions on issues, including energy policies.

9. Public interest groups may perform different political functions (initiatory, aggregative, communications) with respect to a given set of issues.

10. New types of public interest organizations, mobilizing other types of political attitudes than those represented in such groups at present, could form, as is demonstrated in the analysis of Americans for Energy Independence. The universe of public interest groups ten years from now may look quite different from that of the present.

11. Autonomous groups in a pluralist society may speed up the pace of social change, as is the case with the civil rights movement and the women's movement in America. Thus, public interest groups have the potential of accelerating future movements to change the energy-consumption habits of Americans.

The first ten points have been explained in the foregoing text, but the eleventh point requires some elaboration. Since Rousseau and Tocqueville, sociologists and political scientists have been concerned about the effects of a society's membership-group structure on the nature of its politics. Rousseau thought that membership groups would retard the realization of "the general will," thereby debasing the nature of participation and citizenship. Tocqueville, on the other hand, considered the American tendency to form numerous groups to be a bulwark of American democracy, for he observed that membership in groups taught persons the norms of democracy and that such groups constituted a check against an egalitarian society's possible degeneration into mindless mass conformity. Much of the American political sociology of the 1950s had a decidedly Tocquevillian character. Leading political sociologists, such as Seymour Martin Lipset and William Kornhauser, were preoccupied with explaining the rise of fascism and communism in Europe and the phenomenon of McCarthyism in America.[2] In a manner parallel to that of Tocqueville, they viewed America's interest group structure as protecting American democracy, because membership in groups would teach ordinary Americans the norms of democracy, while the leaders of such groups would fight against possible antidemocratic mass movements. These conclusions were shared by most leading political scientists.

The political sociology of the 1950s emphasized the analysis of the way in which membership groups can slow down and stop social change, conceived by those scholars in terms of undesirable, antidemocratic mass movements. A parallel question not examined was: Under what circumstances might membership groups *promote* social change? In 1971, however, sociologist Maurice Pinard observed that the existence of membership groups enhanced the spread of one mass

---

[2] Seymour Martin Lipset, *Political Man* (Garden City, N.Y.: Doubleday & Company, 1960); William Kornhauser, *The Politics of Mass Society* (Glencoe, Ill.: The Free Press, 1959).

movement—a populist party in Quebec.[3] Certainly the existence of active church organizations and NAACP chapters among middle-class American blacks enhanced the spread of the civil rights movement of the 1950s and 1960s. By 1975, political scientists Jo Freeman and Anne Costain applied the Pinard hypothesis to the social changes initiated by the recent women's movement in America.[4] Thus pre-existing women's groups provided a structure for communicating, discussing, and acting upon the new attitudes concerning social roles which constitute the social change known as women's liberation. Probably this social change proceeded more rapidly in the context of organized women's groups than it would have if such groups had not existed.

Applying the Pinard hypothesis to public interest groups, I consider such groups to have the potential of enhancing social change (government reform and environmentalism, for example). In particular, public interest groups have the potential of speeding up the attitudinal changes which will be necessary if Americans are to conserve significant quantities of energy. Common Cause, the League of Women Voters, the Nader organizations, the Sierra Club, and Americans for Energy Independence already stress the importance of the conservation of energy in their publications and communications. I expect that shortly the federal government will be forced to launch a significant drive for the conservation of energy, because of our still increasing reliance on OPEC oil. In such an eventuality, the leaders of the Federal Energy Administration could cooperate with leaders of public interest groups to persuade the public to change their habits in the direction of the conservation of energy. (Of course the FEA would also need to work toward this end with other groups as well.) While members of public interest groups represent only a small fraction of the overall adult population, these persons tend to be politically active and to be opinion leaders in their home communities. Thus, existing public interest groups have the potential of promoting the attitudinal changes needed to conserve America's supply of energy.

Decisions on Energy: Conclusions

Within the energy field, the following conclusions may be offered about public interest groups.

---

[3] Maurice Pinard, *The Rise of a Third Party* (Englewood Cliffs, N.J.: Prentice-Hall, 1971).

[4] Jo Freeman, *The Politics of Women's Liberation* (New York: David McKay Company, 1975); Anne N. Costain, "A Social Movement Lobbies: Women's Liberation and Pressure Politics." Paper given at the annual meeting of the Southern Political Science Association, November 1975. I am indebted to Anne Costain for pointing out the importance of the Pinard hypothesis.

1. Public interest lobbies have become increasingly critical of nuclear power.

2. No public interest groups analyzed in this study support the development-independence position, except Americans for Energy Independence, which was formed for that specific purpose.

3. Public interest groups will not support the deregulation of the prices of natural gas and of oil, because the constituencies of such groups adhere to the civic-balance system of beliefs. These beliefs imply that the proper role of public interest groups is to *oppose* powerful special interests, a category which includes oil companies.

4. All public interest lobbies support conservation and the development of solar power and of other alternative sources of energy.

5. Nader organizations, which adhere to a particularly strong form of civic-balance beliefs, and environmental lobbies put forth a platform which amounts to a low-energy-growth position. Because they are subject to widespread criticism for doing so, however, such groups are particularly inclined to support solar power and other alternative sources of energy. These groups tend to be particularly concerned about conservation.

6. Common Cause, the League of Women Voters, and Americans for Energy Independence are primarily concerned with policy aggregation. They want to set forth comprehensive energy statements, and thus they give a secondary place to the initiation of specific energy policy proposals.

7. About one-fourth of the members of Common Cause are Republicans or are for other reasons friendly to the interests of business. Because Common Cause (like other public interest groups) makes decisions by consensus, this minority is able to block the adoption of a low-energy-growth position. The mixed-market program of Common Cause embodies a combination of government regulation and price mechanisms and exhibits a concern for development. The League of Women Voters is likely to adopt a similar program, although the league will have difficulty in taking a stand on nuclear power. Both organizations will have difficulty in reconciling the development of coal with environmental values.

8. Public interest lobbies frequently have only limited staffs available for work on questions related to energy. Consumers Union has but one person; the Consumer Federation of America has only two persons. These lobbies with limited staffs must specialize in particular areas of energy policy.

9. Public interest groups initiate policy proposals in areas in which they have a consensus among their supporters. Here is a list of

the groups and the areas in which they perform the function of initiating policy.

a. Common Cause initiates measures concerning the process of decision making in energy policy institutions, including the technique of gaining public commitments during confirmation hearings.

b. Nader organizations were in the second wave of supporters for the proposal for a nuclear moratorium, but Nader can be expected to put forth new proposals concerning the reorganization of the oil industry and the development of solar power.

c. The Sierra Club has creative potential with respect to conservation of energy.

d. Consumers Union initiates lawsuits concerning the pricing of oil and gas.

e. The Consumer Federation of America Energy Policy Task Force set forth the idea of establishing a federally owned oil and gas corporation to compete with private firms.

f. The League of Women Voters has the potential to devise new means of educating the public about energy issues.

g. It is too soon to make such observations about Americans for Energy Independence.

10. As noted above, public interest groups have the potential for gaining public support for the energy-conservation measures necessary to decrease the amount of oil imported by the United States from countries that are members of OPEC.

Americans must get together to formulate policies to deal adequately with the energy shortages now facing us. Public interest lobbies will perform an important function in that process.

APPENDIX A

Questions of Common Cause and Responses of Secretary-designate of the Interior Stanley Hathaway

Conflict of Interest

Question: Will you promulgate recruitment procedures and standards to restrict the number of Interior Department officials with backgrounds in regulated companies and to place individuals with diverse backgrounds in policy-making positions?

Response: I will assure that Department recruitment procedures and standards will restrict, to the maximum extent feasible, the number of Interior officials with experience only in regulated companies. However, the highly technical and specialized nature of several positions may somewhat limit the number of candidates to those whose credentials are primarily related to experience in regulated companies. I will attempt to diversify the background of individuals in policy-making positions.

Question: Will you pledge not to accept employment with regulated companies for at least two years after leaving the Department, and require top officials to do the same?

Response: I consider myself and other Department officials fully bound by applicable law and pledge to comply with it.

Question: Will you require Department officials to divest all financial interests in companies significantly regulated by the Department?

Response: It is my understanding that the Department of the Interior conflict of interest regulations prohibit employees from owning finan-

See *Hearings before the Committee on Interior and Insular Affairs, U.S. Senate, on the Nomination of Stanley K. Hathaway to be Secretary of the Interior: April 21, 22, 30, May 5, 6, 1975* (Washington, D.C.: U.S. Government Printing Office, 1975), pp. 484–87.

cial interests which conflict substantially, or appear to conflict substantially, with the duties they are performing with the Department. These regulations may require changes in assigned duties to non-conflicting positions; divestment of the conflicting interest; disciplinary action; or disqualification for a particular assignment. I will see that the regulations are fully enforced.

Question: Will you require Department officials at GS-15 or above to file public reports covering their financial holdings, outside sources of income, indebtedness, and severance arrangements with former employers?

Response: The Department's conflict of interest regulations require disclosure by Department officials at GS-15 or above, of financial holdings, outside income, indebtedness and severance arrangements where there is a continuing salary. These, however, are not public, but are subject to close scrutiny within the Department by responsible officials and by the General Accounting Office.

Question: What steps will you take to ensure full compliance with the Department's conflict of interest and financial disclosure regulations?

Mr. Hathaway should also be required to submit a detailed personal financial disclosure report to the committee on sources and amounts of his income and financial holdings as well as those of his spouse and any dependent children. This report should be released to the public before the Committee votes on his confirmation.

Response: I recognize that the General Accounting Office analysis disclosed within one of Interior's bureaus apparent shortcomings with respect to compliance of Interior's regulations relating to conflict of interest and financial disclosure. I will insist upon full compliance with the filing, disciplinary and remedial actions provided in the regulations.
[Hathaway complied with the request to release to the public a detailed financial report.]

Leasing Procedures

Questions: Do you favor stronger lease provisions requiring coal and oil companies to develop leased reserves in a diligent fashion, and increased rental and royalty rates with respect to future leases of Federal energy reserves?

Do you favor more competitive bidding procedures on these reserves and the termination of preference right leases?

114

Do you favor the integration of BLM's leasing decisions into a comprehensive land use plan regarding Federal reserves?

Do you believe coal and oil companies should be required to submit to the U.S. Geological Survey, as a condition for obtaining a lease, all their documents with respect to reserves they wish to develop?

What specific regulatory or legislative steps will you take with respect to these reforms?

Responses: The leasing procedures of the Bureau of Land Management and U.S. Geological Survey are of central importance to responsible administration of the natural resources of public lands. My basic philosophy about natural resource leasing is that the Federal government must balance three important forms of responsibilities:

—Responsibility to the consuming public, which will benefit from timely development of valuable resources;

—Responsibility to citizens who might suffer from environmental costs of improper resource development; and

—Responsibility to the taxpayer, who should receive compensation for use of the resource to the full extent provided by law.

These responsibilities are not always easily balanced, but that is the central task faced by the Department of the Interior.

It is my understanding that Federal coal leasing has been under moratorium, with a few minor exceptions, for nearly four years. I will, of course, fully review the state of planning for future coal leasing if I am confirmed. The basic laws under which minerals are leased are under constant consideration for amendment, and this Administration has, I believe, introduced its own sets of amendments for consideration by the Congress in past sessions. In the process of familiarizing myself with the details of these issues, I will pay special attention to requirements for diligent development, comprehensive bidding, land use planning, and the adequacy of resource information possessed by the government.

Logging of Outside Contacts

Question: Will you promulgate a regulation requiring Department officials at GS-15 or above to log all contracts and written material from outside parties on the public record?

Response: I am in agreement with the concept, and do not object to the suggested method of complying; however, before implementing this on a Departmentwide basis, I would like to assess the impact on the Department, in the form of increased paperwork and in related areas.

Openness Issues

Question: What steps will you take to open Departmental proceedings and policy-making to the public?

Response: The law currently requires that the Department conduct public hearings on many of the critical issues under its purview, such as, the Department's position on various environmental impact statements, and proposals to expand areas of outer continental shelf exploration. I further endorse opening policy formulation to the public to the maximum extent practicable.

Question: How will you ensure that the Department's advisory committees fully comply with the Federal Advisory Committee Act, particularly its open meetings and balanced representation requirements?

Response: I will meet these requirements, and, as I understand it, this will involve maintaining close relationship with the Office of Management and Budget to assure that we meet their guidelines in the areas of representation and procedures.

Question: What steps will you take to facilitate public access to the Department's policy-related documents and to ensure complete and timely compliance with Freedom of Information Act requests?

Response: The Freedom of Information Act requires disclosure of Government documents in a timely fashion. I will insist upon adherence to the spirit and intent of that Act.

APPENDIX B
Common Cause Energy Supply and Environmental Program

Energy conservation is the key to the success of any energy program. But successful conservation will not eliminate the need to develop additional energy sources. The Energy Policy Project of the Ford Foundation pointed out that even in its limited growth scenario (1.9% growth per year), energy supply will need to be approximately 28% larger in 1985 than in 1973.

Decisions to increase energy supply will impact heavily on the environment but are a necessary part of a meaningful and realistic energy program. In developing recommendations for an energy supply program, we have reviewed the report of the Energy Policy Project of the Ford Foundation, the Federal Energy Administration's Project Independence Report, and the Committee for Economic Development's "Achieving Energy Independence." We have studied the energy programs set forth by the Administration, the Congressional Democrats, the House Ways and Means Committee, and the House freshman Democrats. Also, we have consulted with numerous environmental and other interest groups.

In developing an energy supply program, it is necessary to weigh source against source, as well as the pros and cons of each source. Our goal is to ensure that increased domestic energy supplies are developed only within a framework of effective environmental standards. The Ford Foundation's Energy Policy Project outlined the supply choices as follows: "We must either make major commitments to at least two of the four troublesome energy sources noted earlier—oil imports, nuclear power, the Rocky Mountain coal and shale, and drilling in the

This memorandum was prepared by the policy research staff of Common Cause for consideration by the governing board, which approved it as a statement of Common Cause policy in April 1975.

Gulf of Alaska and off the East and West Coasts—or we must go ahead with all four on a more moderate scale."

We have endorsed a conservation-oriented oil import quota program. This memorandum addresses the other three potential sources of supply outlined by the Energy Policy Project. Also, the memorandum discusses the long-range supply options now being decided by federal allocation of energy research and development dollars.

Coal Development

The Ford Energy Policy Project reported that "oil and gas may be our scarcest energy sources over the long term. Coal resources are much more abundant, large enough to meet the present level of total U.S. energy use for several hundred years." David Freeman, the Project's Director, recently testified before the House Ways and Means Committee and pointed out that the prospects for increasing the yearly production of natural gas and oil are limited and that "we urgently need to develop a national commitment to enlarging the use of coal that is mined safely and burned cleanly."

There are numerous arguments against expedited coal conversion, but none that cannot be resolved through careful federal planning. First, coal is dirty and expedited coal conversion threatens the Clean Air Act. When coal is burned, sulfur dioxide is released. Low sulfur coal is available, but much of it has low energy potential. Second, coal mining requires a great deal of land. Third, underground mining threatens the health and safety of the miners. Fourth, strip mining does considerable damage to the environment. Fifth, it could take as many as 300,000 new workers to meet the kind of production needed between now and 1985. Sixth, the transportation available to move mined coal to its markets is limited. Increased use of western coal fields may require the construction of new rail lines and cars. Seventh, the coal industry does not have the capital needed to make the multi-billion dollar investments in mines and other essential facilities.

Most of the arguments against coal conversion can be overcome given time and federal encouragement of coal conversion. First, Environmental Protection Administration studies show that the equipment (scrubbers) needed to cleanse sulfur emissions at the source are available and reliable. Second, there has been a significant improvement in the mine accident record since the passage of the Federal Coal Mine Health and Safety Act of 1969. Third, Congress is about to enact a strip-mining law with tough reclamation standards. Fourth, the employment, transportation, and capital constraints on expedited coal conversion provide time to install the technology necessary to ensure that coal is mined safely and burned cleanly.

Common Cause should urge that expedited coal conversion be the favored supply option as long as environmental and safety standards are met. We should argue that coal conversion take place along with the use of scrubbers and enforcement of mine health and safety standards and tough reclamation standards for strip mining. Also, we should support legitimate federal incentives to encourage capital investment in coal mining, conversion, and transportation.

Offshore Oil Leasing

Offshore oil is estimated to constitute 50 to 70% of our total undiscovered reserves according to the National Academy of Sciences. The Ford Foundation reported: "Oil is a relatively scarce domestic resource, and there is no question that offshore oil will become increasingly important." Most experts agree. In the past, development has been off Texas and Louisiana. The Atlantic's Outer Continental Shelf and sites off Alaska and southern California are seen as areas of potential development. The Administration originally announced plans to accelerate offshore development through a 10 million acre leasing program for 1975. This is as much as has been leased over the past 20 years. More recently, the Administration has cut its projection to 5 million acres.

There are several potential environmental problems with the development of offshore oil. Oil spills affect coastal waters that are particularly productive marine habitats. Offshore oil development leads to the need for supporting facilities onshore that could adversely affect local economies and fragile coastal environments. These potential problems can be dealt with through careful planning and monitoring.

Two pro-development policy alternatives are now being debated: (1) the Administration and the energy-related industries favor an accelerated leasing and exploration program directed by Interior, regulated by present law, and carried out by the private sector; and (2) several members of Congress and many governors of coastal states favor a slower, more deliberate program with participation from the states and federal involvement in data-gathering and perhaps exploration.

The arguments for the Administration's accelerated leasing program are based on the adequacy of present law. Secretary Morton opposes new legislation and argues that necessary changes can be made by administrative action, such as a proposed regulation banning joint bidding by major oil companies.

119

Critics of the Administration's proposal point out that little has been done by administrative action in the past and that present practices need substantial reform. They feel that a main problem with present practices is that the federal government has little idea about the true value of resources in undeveloped regions. The government now possesses a great deal of raw data, but only the individual companies possess the ability to adequately interpret that data. The government knows considerably less about its resources than the industries that are seeking development rights.

Second, federal leasing practices and lack of industry competition have led to misuse of federal lands and inadequate financial returns to the government. Third, accelerated development will have tremendous effects on onshore development of coastal states without giving the states the time to plan for the development as they are belatedly doing under the Coastal Zone Management Act of 1972. Fourth, the development of offshore oil should be carried out in the context of comprehensive energy policy and that only the least risky acres should be leased first. Neither the oil industry nor governmental planning facilities are capable of intelligently or safely developing 5,000,000 acres in the next few years. Current technology may be inadequate for the new environments in which proposed drilling will occur. A recent General Accounting Office study has concluded that the Administration's plan for accelerated leasing is overly optimistic because of the inevitable lead time before development and shortages of essential equipment, material, and manpower.

Common Cause should support a program of developing our offshore oil resources as long as tough environmental standards are established and enforced. We should argue that we have the time to establish an orderly program of federal data gathering, perhaps through the establishment of a federal yardstick corporation, that allows time and provides money for state planning for onshore development. As a major goal of our executive branch program, Common Cause should support adoption of new federal leasing regulations, designed to ensure adequate competition and environmental planning, by the Bureau of Land Management.

Nuclear Power

The Federation of American Scientists, a critic of nuclear power, recently outlined the political options in regard to nuclear power: "One possibility is to phase out the 50 power plants operating and 29 plants with pending licenses; and cancel the 110 plants with existing or impending construction permits and call off the program. A second possibility is to call a halt to construction after the 200 plants built or abuilding are finished, and to resume construction only under specified conditions. A third possibility is business as usual. A fourth is a speed-up of power plant siting and relaxation of some safety restraints." The Administration has proposed that nuclear licensing be expedited so that 200 new nuclear plants be built by the year 1985.

Proponents of nuclear power point out that it has significant advantages in terms of air pollution and land use. The clean air advantages are especially important in the short run as we learn to burn coal in an environmentally acceptable manner. If the breeder is successfully developed, low cost U.S. uranium resources could meet electric energy needs for thousands of years.

Opponents of nuclear power raise a host of unresolved questions. Are the emergency core cooling systems reliable safety mechanisms? Are nuclear facilities and fuels secure from terrorists? Can we safely store radioactive wastes? What are the risks of the breeder reactor? In addition to fundamental health and safety questions, a matter of prime concern to Common Cause should be the Price-Anderson Act, a law providing a partial federal subsidy of insurance costs and a limited liability for utilities using nuclear power. This subsidy distorts the true cost of nuclear power.

The Ford Foundation report concluded: "We do not advocate an absolute ban on new nuclear plants because the problems posed by using fossil fuels instead are also serious. But a conservation oriented growth policy will provide breathing room so that we can gain a better understanding of nuclear power problems, and reach some better judgments before major new expansions of nuclear power are made."

Common Cause should oppose the issuance of additional construction permits until clear and convincing proof of the safety of nuclear power is presented. All plants operating or with construction permits can be allowed to proceed. We should continue to support nuclear R&D funds but at a level lower than that requested by the Administration, thus releasing money for more attractive sources. We should oppose continuation of the indemnity protection afforded the nuclear industry by the Price-Anderson Act.

Research and Development Funds

In the post-1985 period, given adequate research and development funding, conventional fuels could be supplemented by cleaner, renewable energy sources—solar, geothermal, wind, etc. The newly created

Energy Research and Development Administration (ERDA) will receive $3.9 billion in the Administration's FY1976 budget. This is a 20% increase above last year's figures for the same programs.

Unfortunately, the ERDA budget is not consistent with the Common Cause priorities suggested above. Over 78% of the ERDA budget is related directly to nuclear energy. The controversial fast breeder reactor is to receive $443.7 million but only $175 million is requested for the less dangerous fusion option. 30% of ERDA's funds will be spent for national security—weapons, laser fusion, and nuclear materials security. Direct research and development into nonnuclear energy alternatives—coal, solar, geothermal—account for only 10% of the ERDA budget. Less than 1% of the budget will go toward finding ways to use energy more efficiently.

While research and development for new sources do not offer a short range solution to the supply problem, Common Cause should monitor the use of energy R&D funds because of their critical importance for the future. We should advocate a reduction of the nation's commitment to nuclear fission (especially the breeder) and an increase of funds for alternative sources (especially solar and geothermal). Also, research must be increased on pollution control, supply technology, and conservation methods.

As we have said, conservation is the key in the short run. Coal and offshore oil should be our favored supply options but they are a few years off. In the short term, we probably cannot cut off any present sources and this includes nuclear power. But we should urge the government to give detailed and serious study before accelerating nuclear power development. For the long run, we should advocate a shift of priorities in the energy R&D budget from the breeder to alternative sources such as solar and geothermal energy.

APPENDIX C
Common Cause on Nuclear Power

Memorandum on the Nuclear Power Issue, July 24, 1975

Nuclear power is a tremendously complex and controversial subject. The Common Cause position on nuclear power that was approved by the National Governing Board on April 26, 1975, has generated a number of communications from members and friends of Common Cause and outside interest groups, some in support and some in opposition to our position. The purpose of this memorandum is to review: (1) the Common Cause position on nuclear power, (2) the staff's continuing efforts to study all points of view on this issue, and (3) the widespread dissatisfaction in the scientific, business, and political communities with the federal government's present nuclear policy.

Common Cause Position. On April 26, 1975, the National Governing Board of Common Cause approved an energy-supply policy paper ("Energy Supplies and the Environment"). The paper pointed out that while energy conservation is the key to the success of any energy program, additional energy sources will be required. The paper stated that our goal is to ensure that future domestic energy supplies are developed within the framework of effective environmental standards.

During Board discussion of the energy/environment issue, some members expressed concern about the paper's recommendations regarding nuclear power. The Board, however, supported the recommendation:

> Common Cause should oppose the issuance of additional construction permits until clear and convincing proof

Common Cause asked me to include essentially the full text of its antinuclear argument, rather than excerpts, in order to forestall misunderstandings of their position. For an introductory presentation of various points of view on nuclear power, the reader can consult *Is Nuclear Power Safe?*, AEI Roundtable, Melvin R. Laird, moderator (Washington, D.C.: American Enterprise Institute, 1975).

of the safety of nuclear power is presented. All plants operating or with construction permits can be allowed to proceed. We should continue to support nuclear R & D funds but at a level lower than that requested by the Administration, thus releasing money for more attractive sources. We should oppose continuation of the indemnity protection afforded the nuclear industry by the Price-Anderson Act.

By letter of May 12 to Representative Morris K. Udall, Chairman of the House Energy and Environment Subcommittee, David Cohen set forth Common Cause's position regarding nuclear power. The Udall Subcommittee is in the process of holding a series of oversight hearings on nuclear power. Cohen specified several fundamental questions about nuclear power that remain unanswered. He stated that: "Common Cause opposed the issuance of additional construction permits for nuclear power plants until clear and convincing proof of the safety and reliability of nuclear power is documented and certified by Congress." Cohen recommended that Congress commission a comprehensive study to provide it and the public with the information necessary to answer the many questions now unanswered.

Common Cause believes that Congress should commission an independent and comprehensive study designed to give Congress an objective analysis of the nuclear power issue. This study could be performed by a body such as Congress' Office of Technology Assessment and should serve as the basis of an explicit Congressional decision regarding the future role of nuclear power. Congress should not make an irrevocable commitment to nuclear power by default.

Staff Analysis. For a general background on energy policy, the staff reviewed the report of the Energy Policy Project of the Ford Foundation, the Federal Energy Administration's Project Independence Report, and the Committee for Economic Development's "Achieving Energy Independence." We have studied the Administration's position and reviewed reports by the former Atomic Energy Commission (AEC), the new Nuclear Regulatory Commission (NRC), the Energy Research and Development Administration (ERDA), the Federal Energy Administration (FEA), and the Environmental Protection Agency (EPA). We have consulted with environmental and industry interest groups. For example, John Gardner recently met with two executives of the Westinghouse Electric Corporation and several members of the staff received a comprehensive briefing from Westinghouse. Such consultations will continue.

Specific reservations about accelerating the nation's commitment to nuclear power should be viewed in the context of our long-term energy supply requirements. In the course of developing a Common Cause energy/environment program, staff has reviewed over fifty energy scenarios prepared by government, industry, foundations and other research organizations. As one might expect, these studies vary substantially in their assumptions about and projections of energy supply and demand. However, a few generalizations relevant to nuclear power seem warranted:

1. There is no doubt that foregoing any major technology, such as the breeder reactor, entails *some* risk of falling short of necessary energy supplies. Nuclear power now provides 2 percent of our energy needs; a representative sample of projections for year 2000 would range from 2 percent to 29 percent. The perceived risk is basically a function of differing expectations about conservation goals and commercial availability of alternative electricity-generating fuels.

2. Projected demand for electricity is the determinant of nuclear power requirements, and there is widespread agreement that electricity needs have been overstated. Nuclear power (i.e., electricity) cannot significantly displace oil and gas fuels. Conversely, alternatives to nuclear power must be suitable for generation of electricity.

3. Responsible estimates suggest that other technologies could substitute for nuclear power in the long term. Such estimates entail heavy use of coal and/or solar/geothermal energy. For example, a Project Independence Task Force on Solar Energy estimated a "best case" of 39 quads of solar energy in 2000—a total which would eliminate the nuclear power requirements of most scenarios.

4. Coal is a pivotal energy source—it can be used to generate electricity and/or substitute for the declining oil and gas reserves that currently meet our liquid and gaseous fuel requirements.

5. Conventional nuclear power, as opposed to the breeder, can only meet short-term energy needs, given the current estimates of uranium reserves. ERDA estimates that "the size of the uranium resource, if used in current light water reactors, is nearly as large as that for the remaining domestic oil and gas resources." Hence, the long-term (2000 and beyond) viability of nuclear power is completely dependent on commercialization of the breeder reactor. Proponents of nuclear power agree that the breeder is significantly more problematic than conventional reactors.

These generalizations, and the data behind them, indicate that a "slow" or "no-growth" approach to nuclear power is not unreasonable, particularly when predicated on: first, a simple requirement that Congress inform itself objectively and thoroughly on the issue before committing itself to accelerated nuclear power development; and second, a recognition that the real issue involves eventual large-scale commitment to breeder reactors.

Finally, the critical importance of energy conservation vis-à-vis nuclear power development must be re-emphasized. The Investor Responsibility Research Center, an organization which counsels major corporate and institutional investors on the social ramifications of their investment policies, concluded in its analysis of the nuclear power issue:

> Over the coming decades, the rate at which demand for energy increases is the factor likely to exert the strongest influence over development of nuclear power. If growth in energy use continues at anything approaching historic rates, nuclear power will have to play a major role in the energy economy, because it seems clear that other sources of energy cannot be expanded at the rate required to meet the needs that would develop. On the other hand, if growth in demand declines dramatically a limiting of construction of new nuclear power plants beyond those currently on order or planned could take place without unduly constraining energy supply.

With this perspective, we can review the specific issues regarding nuclear power that concern Common Cause:

Nuclear plant safety. The problem here is assessing and accepting the risk of accidental release of radioactivity from a nuclear reactor. Proponents frequently point to 1500 reactor years of safe operation. However, that total includes operation of small military reactors, submarines and aircraft carriers, and civilian power plants far smaller than those being constructed today or planned for the future. Only 12 nuclear power plants operating in 1974 were 800 megawatts or larger in size, and their combined operating time represents only 38 reactor years.

Proponents of nuclear power cite a draft report commissioned by the AEC and directed by Norman Rasmussen of MIT. Rasmussen predicted one major nuclear melt-down every 175 years. The report's methodology and conclusions have been questioned in a 170-page rebuttal prepared by the Union of Concerned Scientists and the Sierra Club. For example, UCS pointed out that as applied to the Apollo fourth-stage rocket engine, Rasmussen's methodology showed a predicted reliability of one failure per 10,000 missions. But the highest level of reliability achieved was four failures for each 100 missions. (The study dealt only with reactor safety. It did not address many of the unanswered questions that trouble Common Cause.)

In 1977, the government will conduct its first actual test of the safety systems of an operating reactor.

Plant reliability/economic viability. The limited operating experience so far with large commercial reactors is also inconclusive with respect to the reliability (i.e., in terms of power generated) and therefore the economic viability of nuclear power. Some data suggest decreasing reliability over time, to the degree that coal plants begin to provide cheaper electricity. The British government decided not to purchase American light-water reactors based on the recommendation of its chief scientific advisor who found that their use "depends on the maintenance of an immaculate standard of manufacture and quality control, and on a regular in-service inspection of the most rigorous and detailed kind."

At present, many defects found in nuclear plants are treated as generic, and therefore their discovery in one plant results in widespread shutdowns around the country. This problem is exacerbated as dependence on nuclear power increases.

American Electric Power Company, the nation's largest privately-held utilities group, plans to rely almost entirely on coal-fired plants. AEP's chairman, Donald Cook, recently remarked that "nuclear plants have more problems than a hound dog has fleas."

Storage and waste disposal. Nuclear reactors produce a variety of wastes with differing levels of radioactivity and life spans. The Natural Resources Defense Council comments that "the environmental and health hazards posed by the generation, transportation and eventual disposal of extremely toxic, long-lived radioactive wastes are unparalleled in the history of man." One of these wastes, plutonium, is one of the most toxic elements known and is considered to present a potential hazard for at least 250,000 years. If breeder reactors come into common usage, the production of plutonium will increase immensely. A breeder reactor will contain a ton of plutonium and will produce seven times as much plutonium as a light-water reactor of equal generating capacity. An energy economy in which breeder reactors play a major role would have three times as much plutonium in circulation as one involving only light-water reactors.

The federal government is responsible for long-term management of nuclear power plant wastes. No method of permanent waste disposal is now operational, and nuclear critics maintain that until such a technology is developed and tested, it is irresponsible to continue producing nuclear wastes. In May [1975], the NRC decided to postpone for at least three years a final decision on whether plutonium should be used to fuel reactors. This was based on concerns raised by an ERDA fuel cycle task force.

Theft and terrorism. Closely related to issues of waste storage, disposal and transportation is the question of illegal diversion and use of nuclear fuels and technology. Terrorists could conceivably build nuclear bombs and radiological weapons, or engage in nuclear black-mail and nuclear sabotage. An AEC task force on safeguards reported in April 1974: "The acquisition of special nuclear materials remains the only substantial problem facing groups which desire to have such weapons." A recent GAO report concluded that current security measures at nuclear power plants could not prevent a takeover by as few as two or three armed individuals. A 1974 study for the AEC by a private consultant (Rosenbaum) found the AEC's existing safeguards for explosive uranium and plutonium in the nuclear power industry were "entirely inadequate" to meet the threat of theft or sabotage. Many government and industry officials concede that safeguards have not always received the attention they deserve, but most contend that times have changed. Nevertheless, disagreement persists on how great the threat of misuse of plutonium actually is; whether adequate safeguards can be developed; what the costs will be and who will pay; and whether safeguards measures will endanger individuals' civil liberties.

International security. All the issues raised above are compounded by the prospect of widespread foreign use of nuclear power. Fourteen foreign nations now have operable nuclear power reactors. By 1980, an estimated thirty countries will have approximately 230 reactors, producing about 65,000 kilograms of plutonium a year. By 2000, these numbers will be, respectively, 3000 reactors, more than one million kilograms, and fifty countries. Experts estimate that India, Japan, Canada, Argentina, Spain, West Germany, Belgium, Italy, the Nether-lands, Britain, Soviet Union, France, China, and possibly Israel have reprocessing capabilities to produce weapons-grade nuclear materials. Reactor sales have been proposed or consummated with Brazil, Iran, South Korea and Egypt. Several of these nations do not belong to the International Atomic Energy Agency. The international security ramifications of this development are apparent and critical.

The significance of these issues is multiplied by the profoundly disturbing dissension surrounding them in the "expert" community.... There is no easy answer to the question of nuclear power. The scientific community is divided. Recently, thirty-two distinguished scientists signed a manifesto that concluded: "We can see no reasonable alternative to an increased use of nuclear power to satisfy our energy needs." Among the signers of this manifesto were seven Nobel

Laureates in Physics. . . . On the other hand, a list of the co-signers of a January 16 [1975] Nader letter criticizing the Administration's proposal for massive nuclear power plant construction indicates the quality of the dissent in the scientific community. . . .

[Conclusion of Memorandum]

The Common Cause position on nuclear power is a responsible one that is well grounded in a review of the arguments on both sides of the issue. The scientific community is divided. People of substance and good will are split. Hard-nosed business investors are beginning to question the economic (let alone the energy) reliability of our commitment to nuclear power. Now is not the time for the government to make an irrevocable commitment to nuclear power. The caution recommended by Common Cause is well justified by the many scientific and economic questions that remain unanswered.

APPENDIX D
Sierra Club Energy Policy

Resolutions passed by the Board of Directors, January 12–13, 1974, in San Francisco:

1. Nuclear Power Policy

The Sierra Club opposes the licensing, construction and operation of new nuclear reactors utilizing the fission process, pending:

    a. development of adequate national and global policies to curb energy over-use and unnecessary economic growth;

    b. resolution of the significant safety problems inherent in reactor operation, disposal of spent fuels, and possible diversion of nuclear materials capable of use in weapons manufacture; and

    c. the establishment of adequate regulatory machinery to guarantee adherence to the foregoing conditions.

(By consensus it was agreed that the above resolution does not apply to research reactors.)

2. Proposed Policy Statement on Offshore Petroleum Extraction

The Sierra Club believes that no offshore petroleum exploration should occur unless and until the following conditions are met:

I

    a. There are adequate mechanisms to control the impacts of onshore support facilities and associated secondary development. Specifically, the Sierra Club calls for amendments to strengthen

---

The material is quoted from a news release, issued by the Sierra Club on January 18, 1974, entitled "Board Actions." Available from the Sierra Club, 324 C Street, S.E., Washington, D.C. 20003.

the Costal Zone Management Act with immediate full funding and implementation of the federal coastal zone management system. Development in adjacent inland areas should conform to state land use plans which must be in effect prior to offshore development. There should be mechanisms to consider energy policy and the siting of on-shore facilities on a regional, interstate basis in areas where several states are adjacent to potential offshore petroleum producing areas.

b. The baseline biological, geological, and environmental data needed to evaluate the future impacts of petroleum development in a prospective area have been obtained.

c. There is adequate funding for studies on the effects of large oil spills and on the cumulative effect of oil pollution on the marine environment.

d. There are readily available in any area subject to oil spills adequate containment and oil recovery systems. There is an urgent need for substantial improvements in this capability, and the Club strongly supports expanded research and development in this area.

e. A comprehensive environmental impact statement under the National Environmental Policy Act has been prepared.

II

Lease sales should be prohibited in areas that possess the following characteristics:

a. high seismic activity, or

b. fragile or unstable geological structures, or

c. proximity to particularly diverse or productive marine ecosystems, or

d. proximity to federal or state marine sanctuaries or areas worthy of inclusion in such systems, or

e. where the visual impact of offshore structures would significantly reduce aesthetic values, or

f. where, by reason of difficult oil-spill containment problems, busy shipping traffic, very deep water, or other factors, the risks are unusually high.

Potential petroleum deposits that lie in such prohibited areas should be held in reserve.

III

In order to permit the public to assess the potential social and environmental costs of petroleum development versus the total value to be realized from petroleum development, there should be no more than a

132

gradual exploitation of offshore oil. Pre-lease sale exploration for off-shore oil prior to development leasing should only be conducted by the government itself, by a quasi-governmental corporation, or through competitive bidding on contracts for that purpose. Subsequent to this exploration, the responsible federal agencies should perform a benefit/cost analysis of the petroleum prospect to determine if leasing is in the public interest. The cost of this program should be recovered through a bidding qualification fee and lease-sale bids.

IV

Petroleum exploration and production that does take place:

    a. must be conducted in accordance with the strictest controls possible under current technology. Specifically we call for:
- (1) regulations to ensure utilization of "highest state of the art" equipment and technology in all phases of exploration, development and production;
- (2) specific stipulations prohibiting ocean dumping of any untreated sewage, oil wastes, drilling chemicals, contaminated formation fluids and any non-inert drilling or production by-products;
- (3) failure mode analysis and systems analysis techniques to assure adequate margins of environmental safety;
- (4) strict regulations eliminating all natural gas flaring, with the exception of minimal safety flares.

    b. must have on-going environmental monitoring programs in active lease areas designed to assess incremental impacts of petroleum development;

    c. must be subject to close surveillance by an adequately staffed and equipped enforcement agency. We call for:
- (1) a significant increase in the technical capabilities of the federal agency responsible for offshore monitoring and surveillance. This should include consideration of transferring responsibility from the U.S. Geological Survey to the EPA.
- (2) expansion of funding to enable the regulatory agency effectively to implement monitoring and environmental safety programs, maintain comprehensive records and continually upgrade staff qualifications and capabilities. . . .

3. Proposed Policy on Oil Shale Development

The Sierra Club opposes any general program to lease federal oil shale reserves for production purposes until research is completed showing that environmental problems can and will be solved or at least reduced to a reasonably acceptable level. . . .

4. Proposed Policy on Energy Research and Development

The Sierra Club urges Congress to provide for the expenditure of at least $2 billion per year for a period in excess of five years for federal research and development, with emphasis in the following areas: geothermal, solar, and fusion power; energy conservation and more efficient utilization of energy; hydrocarbon extraction and conversion problems; stripmining reclamation; nuclear safety; nuclear waste management; biological and medical research related to energy sources; and instrumentation for monitoring pollution.

APPENDIX E
Sierra Club Energy Conservation Ideas

A. Most Important. 1. Change the mandate of "many" federal agencies to eliminate energy promotion and require consideration of energy conservation (examples: TVA, ICC, FAA, FPC, Bonneville Power Administration). Dick Lahn [a committee member] reported that a study identifying the agencies and the language to be changed has already been prepared by the Senate Interior Committee. . . .

2. Establish some type of *high level energy conservation council* to carry out energy conservation planning, forecasting, and monitoring. The need for this council is unclear, pending clarification of the role of the "Conservation Division" of ERDA. The Jackson Bill (SB 2176) sets up a Council (p. 8) and an Office of Energy Conservation. . . .

3. Institute a gasoline tax (conservation tax) on the order of 10¢/gallon the first year, 20¢/gallon the second, and 30¢/gallon the third, including on gasoline for private flying, power boats, recreational vehicles, power tools, etc. To discourage the use of private cars, possibly include some type of rebate of minimal use. . . . The funds would be used for "mass" public transit. Ron Doctor [a committee member] states that Rand studies indicate that a 1 percent gasoline savings per 1¢/gallon tax are likely.

4. Institute minimum private car efficiency standards (to be based on EPA tests, with public release of sales data) for weighted averages per manufacturer.

	Miles per gallon					
1973	1975	1978	1980	1982	1984	1986
12.4	13.6–14.0	18	20	24	28	32

This list of twenty ideas for energy conservation legislation is excerpted from the report of the Energy Conservation Subcommittee as stated in the minutes of the Sierra Club Energy Committee meeting, October 28, 1974. Available from the Sierra Club.

5. Institute federal vehicle taxes based on mileage to discourage purchase of low mpg cars; the following tax schedules are suggested:

Miles per gallon

	less than 10	10–15	15–20	greater than 20	20–25	greater than 25
1975 tax	$500	$250	$100	0		
1980 tax	$1,000	$500	$250		$100	0

6. Institute government take-over of ownership and maintenance of railroad rights-of-way. A major immediate road-bed improvement program should be initiated. The railroad road-beds should be handled as we now handle highways, with the government setting use charges and handling scheduling. The goal is enhanced railroad utilization for passenger and freight service. (An alternate possibility is take-over of the railroads completely.) Bill Futrell [a board member] says that Barry Commoner and a number of environmental organizations are pushing nationalization of railroads.

7. Provide buyers with full energy consumption information for major electricity and gas energy using appliances—refrigerators, freezers, air conditioners, hot water heaters, furnaces. (See S.2176, sect. 8.)

8. Institute federal standards for efficiency of major energy using appliances. (See Calif. A.B. 1575, 25402C, p. 17.)

9. Institute federal program to stimulate state actions to encourage improving insulation in homes, commercial and industrial buildings. Utilize utilities to implement this process. . . .

10. To implement industrial energy conservation:
   a. Change Bureau of Mines procedures to assure collection of energy and use data. Require cooperation with FEA's Office of Environment and Conservation. Require annual reporting of state by state data. . . .
   b. Require FEA and ERDA to collect and publish annually methods used in and results of industrial energy conservation programs . . . including savings and cost, together with economic case studies. . . .

11. Require standardized refillable beer and soft drink containers, basically the Oregon law. . . .

12. To enhance product life, durability and maintainability, require manufacturers of major appliances to provide 5-yr. (or even 10-yr.) full coverage warranties, including free service, parts, and labor.

13. Subsidies of Excessive Energy Use:
   a. The General Accounting Office shall investigate and re-

port the magnitude of depletion allowances, foreign tax credits, drilling expense write-offs, accelerated depreciation, and investment tax credits for each of the major energy industries: petroleum, natural gas, coal, electricity, nuclear. The Office shall examine the post–World War II period, the present and probable future circumstances, and shall indicate the possible ways in which these tax provisions may have benefited the energy industry, owners, managers, and consumers.

[It was quickly pointed out in the full Committee meeting that the Club's policy on the depletion allowance is far beyond this "study" step.]

b. The Environmental Protection Agency shall issue annual reports on the magnitudes and the distribution of the health and other "external" consequences of energy by-products. These reports shall include but not be limited to the consequences of air pollution, mining, transportation accidents, employee health and safety, and consumer health and safety.

c. Continued efforts to get a sulfur tax.

14. Packaging—The Consumer Protection Administration should issue annual reports on the cost and energy dimensions of the major components of final products. These cost components shall include but not be limited to (i) raw materials, food or fiber cost categories, including the portion received by family farm and farm corporation where relevant, (ii) compensation of production, clerical, and managerial employees in the preceding categories, (iii) types of expenses of employees in the preceding categories, (iv) packaging, (v) transportation of finished goods, (vi) indirect business taxes, (vii) interest payments, and (viii) ownership income. Similarly, the energy dimension shall report the BTU consumption in each of these categories, arriving at a total direct energy requirement per unit output.

15. Electric Utility Rate Structures—The Federal Power Commission and the Office of Energy Conservation and Environment in the FEA shall establish a joint committee to promulgate guidelines for rate setting policies by states and utilities. These guidelines shall embody the principle that each class of customer receiving a particular schedule of power should pay those costs associated with the provision of that power. This principle, commonly termed incremental cost pricing, shall be applied within consumer classes, between consumer classes, over the seasons of the year, and between periods of the day. These guidelines shall specifically exclude promotional rate practices between and within consumer classes.

137

B. Less Important. 1. Develop building construction standards involving heat loss, lighting levels, energy use, and implement these for all federal buildings as well as buildings in which federal funds are involved (FHA). . . .

2. Develop and implement information on life-cycle cost for buildings—home and commercial—which includes first and operating costs. Implement these for all federal buildings and buildings in which federal funds are involved. . . .

3. Mandate HUD to upgrade energy of existing public housing.

4. The Department of Agriculture should issue annual reports on the energy used in the production of major food, fiber, and lumber crops. These reports should show such energy use according to (i) major crop or fiber category, (ii) type of energy use, such as equipment or plant operation, irrigation, fertilization, and pest control, (iii) region of the country, (iv) total production and yield per acre, (v) labor input, and (vi) cultivation practices, particularly emphasizing the energy requirements of high energy and low energy practices for producing crops.

5. Ask ERDA to study implementation of total energy packages and to report on their implementation.

APPENDIX F
The CFA Energy Program

The Energy Policy Task Force supports in principle, the following approaches to the Nation's energy problems:

1. Vastly increased government expenditures for energy research and development programs are essential, together with an overall governmental assignment of priorities and allocation of such funds.

2. We urge the promotion and implementation of measures to conserve energy and to use it as efficiently and as wisely as possible.

3. There must be a consolidation within the federal government of the many assignments and responsibilities in the field of energy policy and implementation in a single agency—in addition regulatory responsibilities over energy industries must be consolidated. . . .

4. A more vigorous effort must be undertaken in enforcing antitrust principles with respect to ownership and control over basic alternative energy supplies.

5. Tighter controls are required over the development and exploitation of publicly owned fuel reserves—for example, modification of procedures and terms by which private companies are permitted to find and market petroleum deposits from public lands, both onshore and offshore, must be adopted, and satisfactory procedures for handling geothermal energy and public lands are essential; or, put in different terms, the rights of the public as the owners of valuable resources should be used to accomplish national objectives in the development of those resources.

6. We support and urge the formation of a government owned

This document sets forth the original fifteen-point program of the Consumer Federation of America Energy Policy Task Force, as stated on April 12, 1973, in "Purpose and Policies: Energy Policy Task Force, Consumer Federation of America" (Washington, D.C.: CFA Energy Policy Task Force, 1973).

corporation to engage in finding and developing petroleum deposits and other fuels on publicly held lands.

7. The need for additional much-needed oil refineries and associated facilities requires an action program whereby government—either at the state or Federal levels—will designate suitable sites for the construction of such facilities.

8. There is no longer any justification for a distinction between interstate and intrastate sales of natural gas, and the distinction should be eliminated to the end that a national resource will be regarded and treated as such.

9. Modifications are required in our tax laws to eliminate—or greatly reduce—incentives and inducements for United States petroleum companies to use their resources to look for oil and gas in foreign countries. Under existing policies, it has proved too easy for domestic companies to operate abroad rather than to concentrate their efforts at home.

10. The federal government should continue to provide those rural electric cooperatives serving sparsely settled areas and whose financial situations so requires, loans at a 2 percent interest rate. This recognizes that the good work done by rural electric cooperatives in the past has been through the beneficial interest rates provided by the Federal Government and, as co-ops become strong enough to finance their activities at higher interest rates, they should be expected to do so. But the rural consumers of those cooperatives who simply would not be provided service without the continued beneficial rate cannot be left without electricity.

11. While recognizing that inflation and the costs of environmental concerns have contributed to rising costs in the production of various energy forms, we oppose the proposal to decontrol the wellhead prices for both flowing gas and new gas. Producers of natural gas should not be expected to operate without a satisfactory return on their investment and yet available data suggests that under controlled prices, there has been not only the opportunity, but the actual realization of satisfactory returns for those in the gas producing business. The same monopolistic features of the gas industry which gave rise to the passage of the Natural Gas Act in 1938 still obtain and, in periods of shortage, there is even greater reason to retain control over the rates at which this energy is sold.

12. The mandatory oil import quota system has not achieved its intended goal of preventing United States dependence on foreign sources of oil and should be scrapped. To the extent that a mechanism should be available for controlling the flow of oil imports—if the time ever comes again when it is in the national interest to do so—a

140

tariff arrangement with the funds paid into the United States Treasury is far more desirable.

13. The problems faced by regulators in times of rising costs is not easy. But the protection of the consumer must remain the primary objective of regulation. Accordingly, we believe that any effort to put the consumer at a disadvantage, for example, by basing rates for wholesale sales of electricity on speculative estimates of future costs rather than actual historical costs is ill advised and should be prohibited.

14. Who is appointed to regulatory agencies can have a significant impact on policies adopted and, particularly in time of rising costs, it is essential that those agencies have at least some members with a background in consumer activities and a reputation for concern for the consumer—this is important not only to provide a balance in the deliberations of such agencies, but to assure the public that the opportunity for balance exists.

15. There should be available a consumers' counsel to provide effective advocacy on behalf of the consumer in proceedings before government agencies where policy decisions and important implementing decisions are being made that have an impact on the consumer.

126681

WITHDRAWN

LIBRARY
OF
MOUNT ST. MARY'S
COLLEGE
EMMITSBURG, MARYLAND

APR 22 1977

Cover and book design: Pat Taylor